# Understanding PDA Autism in Teens

## Supporting Independence, Identity, and Growth during Adolescence

Len Jehu

# Table of Contents

# Introduction

Welcome to a journey that is uniquely yours. Living as a teen with Pathological Demand Avoidance (PDA) is not easy, and it often feels like you're navigating a world full of demands that don't make sense or that seem impossible to meet. You've probably heard a lot of things about what PDA is or what it means for you, and maybe some of that feels true, but maybe some of it doesn't quite fit. This book is here to help you make sense of your experience and offer you the tools you need to take charge of your life. It's not about telling you what you should do—because, let's be real, you've heard enough of that. Instead, this is about understanding yourself better, learning new strategies that actually work for you, and finding ways to thrive, even when life feels overwhelming.

PDA in adolescence brings its own set of challenges, but it also comes with opportunities for growth, independence, and empowerment. Whether you've just recently learned about PDA or you've been navigating it for a while, this book will offer insights, support, and practical strategies that are designed with your specific needs in mind. You're not alone in this journey, and the more you understand about how your brain works, the more you'll be able to manage the demands and stresses of daily life.

This introduction will help you understand why PDA shows up differently during your teenage years and how this book will change the way you view the challenges that come your way. Let's begin by exploring why adolescence can feel like such a turning point for teens with PDA and why your experience of the world might feel different from others.

## Why PDA is Different in Adolescence

If you've been living with Pathological Demand Avoidance for a while, you've probably noticed that things have changed a lot since you entered your teen years. The demands of everyday life seem to have multiplied—there's more pressure to do well in school, maintain friendships, think about your future, and maybe even take on new responsibilities at home. All of this can feel overwhelming, and the strategies that might have worked for you when you were younger suddenly don't seem as effective. This is because PDA often presents itself differently during adolescence.

One of the reasons PDA feels different during your teenage years is because of the **increase in expectations and demands**. As a child, you may have had more flexibility to avoid certain demands, or the adults around you might have been more accommodating of your needs. But as you grow older, the expectations placed on you tend to increase. You're expected to take on more responsibilities, whether it's managing your schoolwork independently, making plans for your future, or navigating complex social dynamics. These increased expectations can trigger a greater sense of anxiety and avoidance, making it feel like everything is spiraling out of control.

In addition to the rise in expectations, **adolescence is a time of significant brain development**, which also affects the way PDA shows up. Your brain is going through massive changes, especially in areas related to decision-making, impulse control, and emotional regulation. For teens with PDA, these changes can make it even harder to cope with demands, as your brain may respond to pressure and stress more intensely. The fight, flight, or freeze response, which is a hallmark of PDA, can become more pronounced during your teenage years, making it harder to manage even small requests or challenges without feeling overwhelmed.

Another reason PDA feels different during adolescence is the **social aspect of teenage life**. Friendships, relationships, and social dynamics become more complicated, and there's often a lot of pressure to fit in or meet social expectations. For teens with PDA, these social demands can be just as overwhelming as academic or family demands, leading to anxiety, avoidance, or even feelings of isolation. You might find yourself struggling to maintain friendships because of the pressure to engage in certain social activities or meet the unspoken expectations that come with being part of a group.

The **desire for independence** is another big factor that makes PDA different in adolescence. As a teenager, you naturally want to take control of your own life, make your own decisions, and assert your independence. But for teens with PDA, this desire for independence can sometimes clash with the anxiety that comes from facing demands. You might feel stuck between wanting to take charge of your life and feeling overwhelmed by the responsibilities that come with it. This can create a push-pull dynamic, where you crave control but also feel paralyzed by the expectations placed on you.

Finally, **hormonal changes** during adolescence can heighten emotional sensitivity and anxiety, which can exacerbate the symptoms of PDA. You may find that your emotions feel more intense or that you're more easily triggered by demands or stressors than you were in the past. This emotional intensity can make it harder to cope with the challenges of teenage life, leaving you feeling like you're constantly on edge or unable to relax.

Understanding why PDA is different during adolescence is the first step toward managing it more effectively. By recognizing the unique challenges that come with being a teen with PDA, you can start to develop strategies that help you navigate this stage of life with more confidence and control. In the next section, we'll explore how this book will offer you new ways of looking at the challenges you face and how it can help you build a toolkit for success.

## How This Book Will Change the Way You See Challenges

If you're reading this book, it's probably because you've felt overwhelmed by the challenges that come with PDA. Maybe you've been frustrated by your inability to keep up with the demands of school, or you've struggled to maintain friendships because of the anxiety that social interactions create. Perhaps you've even felt misunderstood by those around you—like people don't really get what you're going through, or they expect you to just "get over it" and deal with things like everyone else does. This book is here to show you that there's a different way to approach those challenges, one that's tailored to your unique experience as a teen with PDA.

The truth is, living with PDA means that you experience the world in a different way, and that's okay. But it also means that the traditional strategies for dealing with demands, stress, or anxiety might not work for you. That's where this book comes in. Instead of trying to fit you into a mold that doesn't align with how your brain works, this book will help you develop tools and strategies that work for **you**—strategies that take into account your need for control, your desire for independence, and the ways that anxiety affects your ability to meet demands.

One of the ways this book will change the way you see challenges is by helping you **reframe how you think about demands**. Right now, it might feel like every demand—whether it's something small like doing your homework, or something big like planning for your future—is a threat that needs to be avoided. But by understanding how your brain processes demands, you can start to shift your perspective. Instead of seeing demands as something you need to run from, you'll learn how to break them down into manageable steps, take control of the situation, and approach challenges in a way that feels less overwhelming.

This book will also help you **develop practical strategies** for managing the anxiety that comes with PDA. Whether it's learning how to manage your time more effectively, setting boundaries that protect your mental health, or finding ways to communicate your needs to others, the tools in this book are designed to help you reduce the overwhelm and regain a sense of control. You'll learn how to create routines that support your well-being, how to balance screen time with real-life responsibilities, and how to navigate the social pressures of teenage life without feeling like you're constantly drowning in expectations.

Another way this book will change how you see challenges is by helping you **build resilience**. Living with PDA can sometimes make it feel like every setback is a disaster, and it's easy to get stuck in a cycle of avoidance when things don't go according to plan. But resilience is about learning how to bounce back from setbacks, even when things feel hard. This book will guide you through the process of building resilience, so you can face challenges with more confidence and less fear. You'll learn how to handle transitions, cope with uncertainty, and develop the flexibility needed to navigate a world that's always changing.

One of the most important things this book will teach you is how to **embrace your strengths**. PDA doesn't define who you are—it's just one part of your story. You have unique strengths and talents that can help you navigate life's challenges, and this book will help you discover and embrace those strengths. Whether it's your creativity, your ability to think outside the box, or your deep sense of empathy, you'll learn how to harness these qualities to overcome obstacles and create a future that excites you.

Finally, this book will help you **redefine success on your own terms**. For teens with PDA, success doesn't have to look like meeting every demand perfectly or fitting into a rigid set of expectations. Success can mean finding balance in your life, managing your anxiety in a healthy way, and making choices that feel right for you. By the end of this book, you'll have a clearer sense of what success looks like for you, and you'll have the tools you need to achieve it.

# Chapter 1

# Cracking the Code – What is PDA in Teens?

Living as a teenager with Pathological Demand Avoidance (PDA) can often feel like a continuous struggle. Imagine being overwhelmed by even the simplest of requests. While it may appear to others that you're being uncooperative, there's a much deeper reason behind these behaviors. PDA is more than just refusing to follow instructions or appearing indifferent; it's a defense mechanism rooted in anxiety. Understanding PDA as a teen is about cracking the complex code of your brain, emotions, and behaviors, and figuring out why everyday tasks and interactions can seem so overwhelming.

PDA is a subtype of autism that revolves around avoiding demands because they trigger intense feelings of anxiety. In teens, this can be misunderstood as laziness, rebellion, or an uncaring attitude. However, it's essential to recognize that PDA isn't about not wanting to do things—it's about not being able to because of the anxiety linked to those demands. When you learn what PDA is and how it affects your life, you can start to make sense of your experiences and begin to explore strategies to cope and thrive.

One of the major challenges for teens with PDA is that people around them often don't understand why they react to requests in such an intense way. You might hear comments like, "You're just being difficult" or "Why don't you try harder?" This can be frustrating and hurtful because, deep down, you know it's not about defiance or lack of effort. Cracking the code of PDA starts with acknowledging that your reactions stem from anxiety—not stubbornness or a lack of discipline.

By grasping the concept of PDA, you can also begin to build more self-compassion. It's easy to get down on yourself when you feel like you're constantly struggling with simple things. But recognizing that your brain is wired differently can help you approach these challenges with more patience and understanding. Instead of thinking, "Why can't I just do it?" you can shift to asking, "What's making this task feel so impossible right now?"

Understanding PDA is also about realizing that you don't have to manage it alone. Building a support system of friends, family, and educators who understand PDA can make a world of difference. When others know that your avoidance comes from a place of anxiety, not defiance, they can help create an environment where you feel less pressure and more understanding. This chapter will guide you through the process of understanding your unique brain and how you can navigate life with PDA in a more empowered way.

## The Science Behind PDA: Why Your Brain is Wired Differently

PDA is closely connected to how your brain processes anxiety. Imagine your brain is always on high alert, constantly scanning for potential threats—even in situations that seem perfectly normal to others. When someone makes a demand, no matter how small, your brain may interpret it as a threat, triggering a fight, flight, or freeze response. This doesn't mean that there's something wrong with you; instead, it's your brain's way of protecting you from what it perceives as overwhelming pressure.

The amygdala, the part of the brain responsible for handling fear and anxiety, is particularly sensitive in people with PDA. This means that tasks or demands that others might handle with ease can feel extremely overwhelming to you. It's like your brain is constantly on overdrive, interpreting everyday requests as too much to handle. For teens, this can create an enormous amount of stress, especially when people around you don't understand why simple tasks feel like monumental challenges.

It's important to recognize that PDA is not a matter of defiance or unwillingness to participate in life. It's more about the brain's response to anxiety and stress. When you're asked to do something—whether it's schoolwork, chores, or social interactions—your brain may react as if it's facing a threat. This heightened response leads to the avoidance behaviors that are characteristic of PDA, and it's essential to understand that these behaviors are a form of self-protection, not a refusal to cooperate.

For many teens, the constant barrage of demands—whether from school, home, or friends—can feel suffocating. This is because your brain is wired to interpret these demands as overwhelming, and your natural reaction is to avoid them to prevent the anxiety from escalating. But while avoidance might bring temporary relief, it can also lead to increased misunderstandings and frustration from others who don't realize the internal battle you're facing.

By learning more about how your brain works, you can begin to develop strategies to manage the anxiety that comes with demands. It's also helpful to educate those around you about how PDA affects your brain, so they can better understand why you respond the way you do. This knowledge can help build more compassionate relationships and reduce the pressure you feel in everyday situations.

In the following sections, we'll explore how PDA shows up in your daily life and how you can begin to move past the misunderstandings that often accompany this condition. Understanding the science behind PDA is the first step in learning to live with it more effectively and with less stress.

## How PDA Shows Up in Everyday Life

If you have PDA, you've probably noticed that it affects almost every part of your life. From school to home to your social life, PDA can make even the most basic tasks feel overwhelming. For many teens, this means struggling to complete homework, avoiding chores, or feeling like they're constantly clashing with parents and teachers. But PDA doesn't just show up in big tasks—it can affect the smallest things, like getting dressed in the morning or deciding what to eat for breakfast.

One of the most common ways PDA manifests is through procrastination. You might find yourself putting off tasks for as long as possible, not because you don't want to do them, but because the anxiety surrounding the demand feels unbearable. This can lead to a cycle of avoidance, where the longer you put something off, the more anxious you feel about doing it, and the harder it becomes to start.

In social situations, PDA can make it difficult to engage with others. You might avoid going to social events or participating in group activities because the demands of interacting with others feel too overwhelming. This can lead to isolation and feelings of loneliness, especially when your friends don't understand why you're pulling away. It's important to remember that this avoidance isn't a reflection of your feelings about your friends or family—it's a way of coping with the anxiety that comes with demands.

At home, PDA can cause tension with family members who don't understand why you're avoiding certain tasks.

You might find yourself arguing with your parents about chores, homework, or other responsibilities. It can feel like they're constantly pushing you to do things that you just can't manage, which can lead to frustration on both sides. But by recognizing that your avoidance is a response to anxiety, not a refusal to cooperate, you can begin to find ways to manage these conflicts more effectively.

In school, PDA can make it challenging to keep up with assignments, participate in class, or follow a routine. You might feel like you're constantly falling behind or struggling to meet expectations, which can lead to increased stress and anxiety. It's important to communicate with your teachers about your needs and find strategies that allow you to manage your workload in a way that feels more manageable.

Understanding how PDA shows up in your everyday life is the first step in learning to manage it. By recognizing the patterns of avoidance and the situations that trigger your anxiety, you can begin to develop strategies to cope with these challenges more effectively. In the next section, we'll explore how to move past the misunderstandings that often come with PDA and start building more supportive relationships with the people around you.

## Moving Past the Misunderstandings

Teens with PDA often face a lot of misunderstandings from the people around them. Because PDA isn't as well-known as other forms of autism, many people don't understand why you react the way you do to everyday demands. This can lead to frustration and tension in your relationships, as others might see your avoidance as laziness, defiance, or a lack of effort. But moving past these misunderstandings is possible, and it starts with education and communication.

The first step in moving past misunderstandings is helping others understand what PDA is and how it affects you. This might mean having conversations with your parents, teachers, and friends about what triggers your anxiety and why certain tasks feel overwhelming.

By explaining that your avoidance is a response to anxiety, not a lack of willingness, you can begin to change how others perceive your behavior.

It's also important to recognize that many people aren't familiar with PDA, so it might take time for them to understand what you're going through. Patience is key in these situations, both with yourself and with others. While it can be frustrating when people don't immediately get it, it's important to remember that building understanding takes time and effort on both sides.

One of the most effective ways to move past misunderstandings is to work on developing strategies that help you manage your anxiety and communicate your needs more clearly. This might involve working with a therapist, counselor, or trusted adult who can help you develop coping mechanisms and improve your communication skills. By learning how to express your feelings and needs in a way that others can understand, you can begin to build more supportive relationships.

It's also helpful to set boundaries and find ways to advocate for yourself in situations where you feel overwhelmed. This might mean asking for more time to complete tasks, requesting accommodations at school, or simply letting others know when you need a break. By taking control of your needs, you can reduce the pressure you feel in everyday situations and prevent misunderstandings from escalating into conflicts.

Moving past misunderstandings isn't just about educating others—it's also about building self-awareness and self-compassion. Recognizing that your avoidance behaviors are a response to anxiety, not a personal failing, can help you develop a more positive relationship with yourself. This self-understanding is key to managing PDA and living a more fulfilling life.

# Chapter 2

# Turning Conflict into Connection

Conflict is a normal part of life, but for teens with PDA, it can feel like a constant battle. Whether it's with parents, teachers, or friends, conflicts can arise quickly and escalate into full-blown arguments. But while conflict is often seen as negative, it can actually be an opportunity for growth and connection. The key is learning how to navigate these moments in a way that fosters understanding rather than division.

For teens with PDA, conflicts often stem from the anxiety triggered by demands. When you feel overwhelmed by a request, it's easy for frustration to turn into anger, leading to arguments that feel impossible to resolve. But by understanding the root of your reactions and learning how to communicate more effectively, you can begin to turn these conflicts into opportunities for deeper connection with the people around you.

We'll explore why conflicts happen, how to decode the triggers that lead to arguments, and how you can use these moments as opportunities to build stronger, more supportive relationships. By learning to navigate tough conversations without meltdowns, you can transform your relationships and reduce the stress that comes with conflict.

## Why Conflicts Happen: Decoding the Triggers

For teens with PDA, conflicts often happen because of the intense anxiety triggered by demands. When someone asks you to do something that feels overwhelming, your natural reaction might be to push back, argue, or shut down completely. This can lead to misunderstandings and arguments, especially when the person making the request doesn't understand why you're reacting this way.

One of the most important steps in managing conflict is decoding the triggers that lead to arguments. This means identifying the specific demands or situations that cause your anxiety to spike. For some teens, it might be the pressure of meeting deadlines at school, while for others, it could be the tone of voice a parent uses when making a request. By understanding what triggers your anxiety, you can begin to anticipate conflicts before they happen and work on strategies to manage your reactions.

It's also important to recognize that not all demands are created equal. Some demands might feel more overwhelming than others, depending on the context and your emotional state at the time. For example, being asked to do homework after a long day at school might feel like too much, while the same task might be manageable on a day when you're feeling more relaxed. By paying attention to how your triggers fluctuate, you can begin to develop a more nuanced understanding of your reactions.

Decoding your triggers also involves being aware of your physical and emotional responses in the moment. When you feel your anxiety rising, it's important to recognize the signs early on—whether it's a racing heart, shallow breathing, or a feeling of overwhelm. By catching these signs early, you can take steps to calm yourself before the conflict escalates.

Once you've identified your triggers, the next step is learning how to communicate them to others. This can be challenging, especially if you're used to avoiding conflict or shutting down in stressful situations. But by explaining your triggers and how they affect you, you can help others understand why certain situations lead to conflict and work together to find solutions that reduce stress.

In the following section, we'll explore how to turn arguments into opportunities for bonding and how to navigate tough conversations without letting them spiral into meltdowns. Understanding your triggers is the first step in managing conflict and building stronger, more supportive relationships.

## Turning Arguments into Opportunities for Bonding

It might sound surprising, but conflicts don't always have to be negative. In fact, arguments can be an opportunity for bonding and growth—if they're handled in the right way. When you and the person you're arguing with take the time to understand each other's perspectives, you can use the conflict as a way to build a stronger connection.

One of the most important things to remember during an argument is that it's not about winning or losing. Instead, focus on using the conflict as a way to learn more about yourself and the other person. Ask yourself, "What can I take away from this situation that will help me grow?" By shifting your mindset from one of confrontation to one of curiosity, you can begin to see conflicts as opportunities for deeper understanding.

During an argument, it's easy to get caught up in the heat of the moment and react emotionally. But by taking a step back and focusing on the underlying issue—whether it's the anxiety triggered by a demand or a misunderstanding—you can start to address the root cause of the conflict rather than just the surface-level argument.

Another key to turning arguments into bonding opportunities is active listening. Instead of focusing on defending yourself or proving your point, take the time to really listen to what the other person is saying. This not only helps you understand their perspective, but it also shows them that you're willing to engage in the conversation with empathy and an open mind. In turn, this can help de-escalate the situation and create a space for more meaningful communication.

When you approach conflicts with the goal of understanding rather than winning, you can use them as a way to build trust and deepen your relationships. By focusing on the emotions behind the argument—whether it's fear, frustration, or anxiety—you can create a space where both you and the other person feel heard and validated.

Turning arguments into opportunities for bonding isn't easy, especially when emotions are running high. But with practice, you can begin to shift the way you handle conflicts and use them as a tool for growth and connection.

## Navigating Tough Conversations Without Meltdowns

One of the biggest challenges for teens with PDA is navigating tough conversations without feeling like you're spiraling into a meltdown. These moments, when emotions are high and it feels like everything is out of control, can be incredibly overwhelming. But there are strategies you can use to manage these conversations without letting them escalate into full-blown meltdowns.

The first step in managing tough conversations is recognizing when you're starting to feel overwhelmed.

This might be a physical sensation, like a tightness in your chest or a racing heart, or it could be an emotional response, like frustration or anxiety. When you notice these signs, it's important to take a step back and give yourself a moment to regroup.

One strategy that can be helpful in these situations is taking a break. If you feel like you're about to lose control, ask for a few minutes to step away from the conversation and collect your thoughts. This gives you a chance to calm down and come back to the conversation with a clearer mind. It also shows the other person that you're taking responsibility for managing your emotions, which can help de-escalate the situation.

Another key to navigating tough conversations is practicing mindfulness. When you feel like a conversation is getting heated, focus on your breathing and try to stay present in the moment. This can help prevent your emotions from spiraling out of control and allow you to stay grounded during the conversation.

It's also important to set boundaries during tough conversations. If you feel like a demand is too overwhelming, it's okay to let the other person know that you need some time to process before responding. This can help prevent the conversation from escalating and give you the space you need to manage your anxiety.

By using these strategies, you can begin to navigate tough conversations with more confidence and less stress. While it may take time and practice, learning to manage your emotions during conflicts can lead to more positive, productive conversations and stronger relationships.

# Chapter 3

# Building Independence, Your Way

As a teen with Pathological Demand Avoidance (PDA), the idea of independence can feel like a double-edged sword. On one hand, you crave the freedom to make your own choices and live life on your own terms. On the other hand, the overwhelming pressure to meet expectations and handle responsibilities can make the journey toward independence feel impossible. It's important to recognize that independence doesn't have to look the same for everyone, especially when you're navigating life with PDA.

Independence for a PDA teen is about finding the balance between being able to do things on your own while also understanding your limits and what causes you anxiety. It's not about fitting into a rigid definition of independence, but rather about creating your own path—one that works for you. This chapter will guide you through what independence really means when you have PDA, how to break free from the pressure without feeling overwhelmed, and how to take small, meaningful steps toward bigger victories in your daily life.

Embracing independence isn't about trying to be someone you're not. Instead, it's about figuring out what works best for your unique brain and your personal needs. It's also about learning to navigate the expectations of others—parents, teachers, and friends—while staying true to yourself. As you read through this chapter, remember that your journey toward independence is a personal one, and it's okay to take it at your own pace.

## What Independence Really Means for PDA Teens

For most teens, independence is seen as a rite of passage—an expected part of growing up. But for teens with PDA, independence can feel like an overwhelming challenge, especially when it seems like everyone else around you is handling it with ease. It's important to understand that independence doesn't have to be a one-size-fits-all experience. What works for someone else might not work for you, and that's okay.

Independence for PDA teens isn't about being able to do everything on your own or meeting all the demands placed on you. Instead, it's about learning how to manage your anxiety and avoid feeling overwhelmed while still finding ways to do the things that matter to you. This could mean taking small steps toward independence, like learning how to make your own decisions or managing your time more effectively. It's about figuring out what you need to feel comfortable and confident in your ability to handle life's challenges.

One of the biggest misconceptions about independence for PDA teens is that it means being completely self-sufficient. In reality, independence is about knowing when to ask for help and when to rely on others for support. This doesn't make you any less independent—it simply means that you're aware of your limits and are taking steps to manage your anxiety in a healthy way.

It's also important to recognize that independence is a journey, not a destination. You don't have to become fully independent overnight, and it's okay to take your time as you figure out what works best for you. There's no rush to get there, and it's important to celebrate your small victories along the way.

For teens with PDA, independence is about finding a balance between doing things on your own and understanding when you need support. It's about creating a life that works for you and doesn't feel overwhelming. As you continue on your journey toward independence, remember that you have the power to shape your own path.

In the following sections, we'll explore how you can break free from the overwhelming pressure of independence, how to take small steps toward big wins, and how to build a life that works for you—on your own terms.

## Breaking Free Without Feeling Overwhelmed

One of the biggest challenges for teens with PDA is the constant feeling of being overwhelmed. The pressure to meet expectations and handle responsibilities can make the idea of independence seem impossible. But breaking free from this pressure doesn't mean ignoring your responsibilities—it means finding ways to manage them in a way that doesn't cause you anxiety.

The first step in breaking free from the feeling of being overwhelmed is to recognize that it's okay to ask for help. Independence doesn't mean doing everything on your own—it means knowing when to rely on others for support. This could mean talking to a trusted friend, family member, or therapist about the challenges you're facing and finding ways to work through them together.

Another important step is learning how to manage your time effectively. For teens with PDA, time management can be a major source of anxiety, especially when it feels like there's never enough time to get everything done.

Breaking tasks down into smaller, more manageable steps can help reduce the feeling of being overwhelmed and make it easier to focus on one thing at a time.

It's also important to set boundaries and know your limits. Independence doesn't mean saying yes to every demand that comes your way—it means knowing when to say no and when to take a step back. This could mean setting aside time each day to relax and recharge, or it could mean letting others know when you're feeling overwhelmed and need a break.

In addition to setting boundaries, it's helpful to create a routine that works for you. This could mean establishing a daily schedule that includes time for both work and relaxation, or it could mean setting specific goals for each day and rewarding yourself for completing them. A routine can help reduce the feeling of being overwhelmed by providing structure and predictability.

Finally, breaking free from the pressure of independence means being kind to yourself. It's easy to get caught up in the idea that you should be able to do everything on your own, but it's important to remember that everyone needs help sometimes. Don't be afraid to reach out for support when you need it, and don't be too hard on yourself if things don't go as planned.

## Small Steps to Big Wins in Daily Life

Building independence doesn't happen overnight—it's a gradual process that involves taking small steps toward bigger goals. For teens with PDA, this process can feel daunting, especially when the demands of everyday life seem overwhelming. But by focusing on small, manageable tasks, you can begin to build your independence in a way that feels empowering rather than stressful.

One of the best ways to start building independence is by setting small, achievable goals for yourself. These could be as simple as getting out of bed on time, completing a homework assignment, or cooking a meal for yourself. Each small step you take toward independence is a win, and it's important to celebrate these victories, no matter how small they may seem.

Another way to build independence is by taking responsibility for your own decisions. This could mean choosing what to wear each day, deciding how to spend your free time, or making choices about your future. By taking ownership of your decisions, you're taking an important step toward independence and showing yourself that you're capable of making good choices.

It's also helpful to practice problem-solving skills in your daily life. This could mean figuring out how to handle a difficult situation at school, finding ways to manage your time more effectively, or coming up with solutions to challenges you're facing at home. Problem-solving is an important part of independence, and the more you practice it, the more confident you'll become in your ability to handle life's challenges.

In addition to setting goals and making decisions, it's important to take care of yourself physically and emotionally. This could mean establishing a routine that includes regular exercise, healthy eating, and plenty of sleep. It could also mean finding ways to manage your anxiety, such as practicing mindfulness or talking to a therapist. Taking care of yourself is an important part of building independence, and it's important to prioritize your well-being as you work toward your goals.

Finally, building independence means learning to trust yourself. It's easy to doubt your abilities, especially when you're facing new challenges. But by taking small steps and focusing on your strengths, you can build confidence in your ability to handle life's demands. Remember that independence is a journey, and it's okay to take your time as you figure out what works best for you.

# Chapter 4

# The School Struggle – Thriving in a Demanding Environment

Navigating school as a teen with Pathological Demand Avoidance (PDA) can feel like an endless uphill battle. School comes with a rigid structure, expectations, and demands that can often trigger anxiety and avoidance behaviors. For teens with PDA, the traditional school system may seem like it's set up against them—homework deadlines, class schedules, participation requirements, and social dynamics can all be overwhelming. However, thriving in school is possible, even in a demanding environment. It's all about finding ways to make the school system work for you, rather than feeling trapped by it.

Thriving doesn't mean you need to fit into a mold or meet every expectation placed on you. It means figuring out strategies that allow you to navigate school in a way that supports your unique needs and strengths. Whether you're struggling with classroom participation, maintaining motivation, or balancing academic pressures with your personal well-being, this chapter will guide you through the steps you can take to survive and even succeed in school.

School can be stressful for any teen, but for those with PDA, it can sometimes feel unbearable. This chapter will help you face the challenges of school head-on by providing practical strategies for avoiding burnout, managing academic pressures, and staying motivated even when it feels hard. Let's explore how you can make school a place where you can thrive, not just survive.

## Facing School Head-On: Making It Work for You

For many teens with PDA, school feels like a place full of demands—demands to perform, behave, socialize, and succeed. When these demands clash with your natural tendencies to avoid pressure, it can lead to anxiety, frustration, and even school refusal. But facing school head-on doesn't mean forcing yourself to fit into a system that doesn't work for you. Instead, it's about finding ways to navigate the school environment that align with your needs and strengths.

The first step in making school work for you is understanding your own limits and triggers. Are there certain subjects or tasks that consistently cause you stress? Do group activities or participation in class discussions feel overwhelming? Identifying these stress points can help you anticipate potential challenges and work on strategies to manage them before they become overwhelming. For example, if participating in class discussions makes you anxious, you can speak to your teacher about alternatives, like contributing through written assignments or speaking one-on-one after class.

Another important step is communicating your needs. If your teachers or school counselors are unaware of your challenges, they won't be able to support you in the ways you need. Having an open conversation about PDA and how it affects your school experience can lead to accommodations or adjustments that make school more manageable. This might involve asking for extra time on assignments, requesting a quiet space to complete work, or working with your teachers to set realistic goals that take your anxiety into account.

It's also essential to build a routine that works for you. School schedules can feel rigid, but finding a routine that balances schoolwork with relaxation and self-care can make a big difference in reducing stress. Set aside specific times for studying, breaks, and hobbies, and try to stick to a schedule that doesn't leave you feeling rushed or overwhelmed. Remember, it's okay to take breaks when you need them—pushing through when you're feeling anxious will only make things harder.

Managing expectations is another crucial part of making school work for you. It's easy to feel like you're falling behind or not meeting the standards that others set, but remember that everyone's journey is different. It's okay to set your own pace and focus on what you can handle. Small victories, like completing a homework assignment or attending a class you were anxious about, are worth celebrating. Don't compare your progress to others—focus on what's right for you.

Finally, don't be afraid to ask for help. Whether it's from a teacher, a school counselor, or a parent, reaching out for support can make all the difference. You don't have to face school alone, and there are people who want to help you succeed.

## Avoiding Burnout in a Rigid System

School can be exhausting, especially when you're constantly feeling overwhelmed by demands. For teens with PDA, burnout is a real risk, especially in a system that often doesn't account for neurodiverse needs. Burnout happens when the stress of managing school responsibilities becomes too much, leading to exhaustion, anxiety, and a feeling of being completely drained. Avoiding burnout requires recognizing when you're starting to feel overwhelmed and taking proactive steps to protect your well-being.

The first sign of burnout is often a sense of dread when it comes to school. If you find yourself feeling anxious or exhausted at the thought of going to school or completing assignments, it's time to take a step back and assess how you're feeling. Ignoring these feelings will only lead to more stress and potential burnout. It's important to recognize when you're reaching your limit and to give yourself permission to take a break.

One way to avoid burnout is by setting realistic goals for yourself. It's easy to get caught up in trying to meet every expectation, but this can lead to feeling overwhelmed and ultimately burnt out. Instead, focus on what's most important and break tasks down into smaller, more manageable steps. For example, if you have a big project due, break it down into smaller tasks that you can complete over several days rather than trying to tackle it all at once.

Another important strategy is learning how to say no. You don't have to take on every extracurricular activity, social event, or school assignment that comes your way.

It's okay to set boundaries and prioritize your mental health. If you're feeling overwhelmed, let your teachers or parents know that you need to scale back on your workload or take a break from certain activities.

It's also essential to build self-care into your daily routine. This could mean taking regular breaks during study sessions, practicing mindfulness or relaxation techniques, or spending time doing things that bring you joy and help you recharge. Self-care isn't a luxury—it's a necessity, especially when you're trying to avoid burnout.

Finally, don't be afraid to ask for support when you need it. Whether it's talking to a counselor about your stress levels, reaching out to a teacher for extra help, or simply confiding in a friend, seeking support can help prevent burnout and make school feel more manageable. Remember, it's okay to ask for help—you don't have to do everything on your own.

In the next section, we'll explore strategies for staying motivated when school feels hard and how you can keep pushing forward, even when the going gets tough.

## Strategies for Staying Motivated When It's Hard

Staying motivated in school can be a challenge for any teen, but for those with PDA, it can feel especially difficult. The pressure to meet academic expectations, combined with the anxiety that comes with demands, can make it hard to stay focused and motivated. However, finding ways to stay engaged with your schoolwork is essential for your success, even when it feels tough.

One of the best ways to stay motivated is by connecting your schoolwork to your personal interests and goals. When you can see how what you're learning relates to your future or to something you're passionate about, it becomes easier to stay engaged. For example, if you're interested in art, try to find ways to incorporate creativity into your assignments. If you're passionate about animals, explore how your science lessons connect to biology or environmental studies. By finding personal meaning in your schoolwork, you can stay motivated even when the material feels challenging.

Setting small, achievable goals is another powerful way to stay motivated. When you're faced with a large project or a long-term assignment, it can be overwhelming to think about completing the whole thing at once. Instead, break it down into smaller tasks and set mini-goals for each day or week. This not only makes the work feel more manageable but also gives you a sense of accomplishment as you check off each goal.

It's also important to reward yourself for your hard work. After completing a difficult assignment or reaching a goal, take time to celebrate your success. This could be as simple as watching your favorite show, spending time with friends, or treating yourself to a snack. Positive reinforcement can help you stay motivated and make school feel less like a chore.

Finding a study routine that works for you is another key to staying motivated. Everyone has different study habits, and it's important to find a routine that fits your needs. Some teens with PDA may find it helpful to study in short bursts with frequent breaks, while others might prefer longer, uninterrupted study sessions. Experiment with different routines until you find one that helps you stay focused without feeling overwhelmed.

Finally, staying motivated means being kind to yourself. It's normal to have off days when you feel unmotivated or frustrated with school. Instead of being hard on yourself, acknowledge your feelings and give yourself permission to take a break or try again tomorrow. Remember, motivation doesn't always come easily, but with the right strategies, you can push through even when it feels tough.

# Chapter 5

# Friendship and Social Life – Breaking the PDA Barriers

Friendships and social life are an essential part of being a teen, but for those with PDA, navigating social interactions can be a complex and often overwhelming experience. Building and maintaining friendships may come with unique challenges, from dealing with anxiety in social settings to managing the pressure of expectations within relationships. However, having strong, supportive friendships is possible—even with PDA.

Friendships offer an opportunity to connect, have fun, and feel supported, but they can also bring up feelings of anxiety, especially when there are demands placed on the relationship. Understanding the dynamics of friendships when you have PDA is the first step in creating relationships that work for you. This chapter will explore the complexities of PDA and friendships, how to establish healthy boundaries in relationships, and how to build lasting friendships without losing yourself in the process.

While friendships may feel tricky at times, they don't have to be a source of constant stress. With the right strategies and understanding, you can build strong connections that allow you to be yourself while still enjoying the benefits of companionship.

## PDA and Friendships: Navigating the Complexities

Friendships are often seen as a natural part of teenage life, but for teens with PDA, they can be anything but straightforward. The anxiety that comes with demands, the fear of rejection, and the need for control can all create barriers to forming and maintaining friendships. However, understanding how PDA affects your social life can help you navigate these complexities and build meaningful relationships.

One of the biggest challenges for teens with PDA in friendships is the fear of being overwhelmed by social demands. Whether it's being asked to attend social events, participate in group activities, or keep up with constant communication, the pressure to meet these expectations can trigger anxiety and avoidance. It's important to recognize that it's okay to set limits in your friendships. You don't have to attend every event or respond to every message immediately. True friends will understand your needs and respect your boundaries.

Another challenge is managing the fear of rejection. Teens with PDA may feel anxious about whether their friends truly like them or whether they're meeting their friends' expectations. This can lead to overthinking, avoidance, or even withdrawing from friendships altogether. It's important to remind yourself that friendships aren't about being perfect—they're about connection, understanding, and mutual respect. You don't have to meet every expectation to be a good friend.

For some teens with PDA, social situations can feel overwhelming because of the unpredictability of interactions. Not knowing how a conversation will go or what will be expected of you can create anxiety. One way to navigate this is by preparing for social situations in advance. This could mean thinking about potential topics of conversation or practicing how to handle certain social scenarios. Having a plan in place can help reduce the anxiety of social interactions.

It's also important to remember that it's okay to have different social needs than your friends. Some teens with PDA may prefer smaller, one-on-one interactions, while others may enjoy being in larger groups. There's no right or wrong way to socialize, and it's important to find what works best for you.

Finally, it's essential to communicate your needs with your friends. If you're feeling overwhelmed or anxious about a social situation, let your friends know. True friends will want to support you and help you feel comfortable. By being open about your needs, you can create friendships that are based on understanding and respect.

## Creating Healthy Boundaries in Relationships

Boundaries are a vital part of any healthy relationship, but for teens with PDA, setting and maintaining boundaries can be especially important. Boundaries help protect your emotional well-being and ensure that your relationships remain supportive rather than overwhelming. However, creating boundaries can feel challenging, especially when you're worried about how others might react.

The first step in creating healthy boundaries is understanding your own needs. This means recognizing what makes you feel comfortable and what causes you anxiety in your relationships. Do you need more space or time to yourself? Are there certain topics or activities that make you uncomfortable? Understanding your needs will help you determine what boundaries to set in your friendships.

Once you've identified your needs, the next step is communicating them to your friends. This can feel daunting, but it's important to remember that setting boundaries isn't about pushing people away—it's about creating relationships that work for both parties. When communicating your boundaries, try to be clear and direct. For example, if you need time to yourself after a social event, let your friends know that you'll be taking a break from texting for the rest of the day.

It's also important to be consistent with your boundaries. If you've set a boundary around not participating in certain activities, try to stick to it, even if you feel pressure to say yes. Being consistent with your boundaries helps reinforce their importance and ensures that your friends understand and respect them.

While setting boundaries is essential, it's also important to be flexible when needed. Relationships are dynamic, and there may be times when you need to adjust your boundaries to accommodate different situations. For example, you might feel comfortable attending a social event one day but need more space on another day. Being flexible with your boundaries allows you to adapt to different circumstances without compromising your needs.

It's also crucial to respect the boundaries of others. Just as you have your own needs, your friends have theirs as well. By respecting their boundaries, you show that you value their well-being and are committed to maintaining a healthy, supportive relationship.

Creating healthy boundaries in relationships can help reduce the anxiety and overwhelm that often come with social interactions. By setting clear, consistent boundaries, you can build friendships that are based on mutual respect and understanding.

## How to Build Friendships Without Losing Yourself

Building friendships is an important part of teenage life, but for teens with PDA, there's often a fear of losing oneself in the process. The pressure to meet social expectations, the anxiety of demands, and the desire to fit in can sometimes lead to sacrificing your own needs or identity to maintain relationships. However, it's possible to build strong, supportive friendships without losing sight of who you are.

The first step in building friendships without losing yourself is staying true to your values and interests. It's easy to feel pressure to conform to what others are doing or to participate in activities that don't align with your interests. However, it's important to remember that true friendships are based on mutual respect and shared values. By staying true to yourself, you attract friends who appreciate and support you for who you are, rather than who they want you to be.

Another important aspect of maintaining your sense of self in friendships is setting boundaries, as discussed in the previous section. Boundaries help protect your individuality and ensure that you're not sacrificing your own needs to meet the expectations of others. By setting and maintaining clear boundaries, you create space for yourself within your friendships, allowing you to nurture both the relationship and your own well-being.

It's also important to find friends who share your interests and values. While it's great to have a diverse group of friends with different perspectives, having at least a few friends who share your passions and hobbies can make it easier to stay connected to your own identity. Whether it's through a shared interest in music, art, sports, or other activities, having friends who understand and support your passions can help reinforce your sense of self.

One of the keys to building friendships without losing yourself is being confident in who you are. It's natural to want to fit in, but it's also important to embrace your uniqueness. Everyone has something special to offer in a friendship, and by being confident in your own strengths and qualities, you can build relationships that are based on mutual respect and admiration.

Finally, remember that it's okay to walk away from friendships that aren't supportive or that make you feel like you're losing yourself. If a friendship is causing you more stress than joy, or if you feel like you're constantly compromising your own needs to maintain the relationship, it might be time to reassess whether the friendship is healthy for you. True friendships should make you feel empowered, supported, and valued for who you are.

# Chapter 6

# Family Life Without the Struggle

Navigating life as a teen with Pathological Demand Avoidance (PDA) can feel overwhelming enough, but when the demands and expectations of family are added to the mix, the stress can be amplified. For teens with PDA, family life often becomes a battleground where simple requests can turn into full-blown conflicts. However, family doesn't have to be a source of constant struggle. With understanding and communication, family life can become smoother and more supportive, providing a foundation where you can grow and thrive.

Your family plays a significant role in your PDA journey. They are often the ones who witness your daily challenges and experience the impact of your avoidance behaviors. This chapter will explore how your family can support you in your PDA journey, how you can work together to reduce tensions and misunderstandings, and how to transform family dynamics so that home life becomes a place of comfort rather than conflict.

It's essential to remember that your family's support can make a huge difference in how you manage your PDA. By building open lines of communication and fostering understanding, you can work together to create a home environment that feels safe and supportive, allowing you to navigate your challenges without the added stress of constant tension. Let's look into how you and your family can work toward a better understanding of each other and reduce the daily struggles.

## Understanding Your Family's Role in Your PDA Journey

Family plays a critical role in your PDA journey, whether you realize it or not. Your parents, siblings, and other close family members are often the people who see you at your most vulnerable. They're the ones who experience your avoidance behaviors, witness your anxiety spikes, and try to make sense of your reactions to everyday demands. While it can sometimes feel like they're adding to the pressure, it's important to understand that, for the most part, your family wants to help—they just might not know how.

When it comes to PDA, many families struggle to understand what it really means. They might interpret your avoidance behaviors as defiance, laziness, or disinterest, which can lead to frustration on both sides. It's important to recognize that misunderstandings are common, especially if your family doesn't fully understand how PDA affects you. This is where open communication comes into play.

One of the first steps toward reducing family tensions is helping your family understand what PDA is and how it affects you. This might mean having a conversation with your parents or siblings about how certain demands make you feel and why you might react the way you do. It's important to explain that your avoidance isn't about refusing to cooperate or being difficult—it's a response to the overwhelming anxiety you feel when faced with demands.

Your family's role in your PDA journey is to provide support and understanding, but they can't do that effectively if they don't know what you're going through. By helping them understand PDA from your perspective, you can begin to shift the dynamic from one of conflict to one of support. This doesn't mean that every disagreement will magically disappear, but it does mean that your family will be better equipped to respond to your needs in a way that feels more supportive and less confrontational.

Another important aspect of your family's role is helping you manage your triggers. If your family is aware of the things that cause you the most stress, they can work with you to minimize those triggers and create a more comfortable home environment. For example, if being asked to complete tasks immediately causes anxiety, your family can try to give you more time or provide options that allow you to feel more in control.

Ultimately, your family's role is to be your support system. They might not always get it right, and there will likely be times when misunderstandings arise, but by working together and communicating openly, you can create a home environment that supports your PDA journey rather than making it more difficult.

## Reducing Family Tensions and Misunderstandings

Family life can be a source of tension, especially when there's a lack of understanding about PDA and how it affects your behavior. Misunderstandings can quickly escalate into arguments, leaving both you and your family feeling frustrated and disconnected. However, reducing family tensions is possible, and it starts with building a foundation of understanding and empathy.

One of the most common sources of tension in families with a PDA teen is the expectation that you should be able to handle demands the same way other family members do. For example, your parents might expect you to complete chores, keep up with schoolwork, or participate in family activities without understanding why these demands cause you so much anxiety. This disconnect can lead to feelings of frustration on both sides—you might feel like your family doesn't understand you, while they might feel like you're not putting in enough effort.

To reduce these tensions, it's important to have open and honest conversations about what triggers your anxiety and avoidance behaviors. Explain to your family that PDA makes certain tasks feel overwhelming and that your reactions are not a reflection of how much you care about them or about the task at hand. By helping your family understand that your avoidance is a response to anxiety, not defiance, you can start to shift the conversation from one of blame to one of understanding.

Another key to reducing family tensions is finding compromises that work for everyone. This might mean working together to create a system where demands are presented in a way that feels less overwhelming to you. For example, if being asked to do something immediately triggers anxiety, you could work with your family to create a schedule or set time limits that allow you to complete tasks at your own pace. This not only reduces the pressure you feel but also helps your family understand that you're still committed to contributing—you just need to do it in a way that works for you.

It's also important for your family to recognize the signs of when you're feeling overwhelmed. If they can spot the early warning signs of your anxiety, they can help prevent situations from escalating into full-blown conflicts. This might involve taking a step back when they notice you're becoming anxious or offering support in a way that feels helpful rather than adding more pressure.

Finally, reducing family tensions requires patience and empathy on both sides. It's easy to get caught up in the frustration of misunderstandings, but it's important to remember that everyone is trying their best. By approaching each situation with empathy and a willingness to understand each other's perspectives, you can create a more harmonious family dynamic that supports your well-being.

## Transforming Family Dynamics for a Smoother Home Life

Family dynamics can be complex, especially when you add the challenges of PDA into the mix. However, with effort, communication, and a willingness to adapt, it's possible to transform these dynamics and create a home environment that feels supportive, understanding, and free from constant conflict.

One of the first steps in transforming family dynamics is setting clear expectations and boundaries. For teens with PDA, demands can feel overwhelming, and the pressure to meet those demands can lead to avoidance or anxiety. By working with your family to establish realistic expectations, you can reduce the stress that comes with daily demands. This might mean setting limits on when and how tasks are assigned or creating a routine that gives you more control over your responsibilities.

It's also important to establish boundaries around communication. Family members might not always understand how their words or tone of voice can trigger anxiety. By setting boundaries around how conversations about demands are approached, you can create a more comfortable environment for everyone. For example, if being asked to do something in a certain way makes you anxious, you can ask your family to approach requests in a more gentle or flexible manner.

Another key to transforming family dynamics is building routines that work for everyone. Routines can provide structure and predictability, which can be helpful for reducing anxiety. Work with your family to establish daily routines that allow you to meet your responsibilities while also giving you the space you need to manage your anxiety. This might mean setting specific times for chores, homework, or relaxation, so you know what to expect each day.

In addition to routines, it's important to focus on creating positive family experiences. When PDA is at the forefront of family dynamics, it's easy for every interaction to feel focused on conflict or demands. To transform this dynamic, make an effort to spend time together as a family in ways that are enjoyable and stress-free. Whether it's watching a movie together, going for a walk, or playing a game, finding ways to connect without the pressure of demands can help strengthen your family bonds.

Finally, transforming family dynamics requires ongoing communication and flexibility. Family life is constantly changing, and what works today might not work tomorrow. It's important to check in with each other regularly, talk about what's working and what's not, and be willing to adapt as needed. By keeping the lines of communication open and remaining flexible, you can create a home environment that supports your PDA journey and allows everyone to thrive.

# Chapter 7

# Handling Pressure Like a Pro – Stress and Anxiety Hacks

Living with PDA as a teen means that pressure and stress can feel like constant companions. The demands of school, friendships, family, and everyday life can pile up, making it hard to catch your breath or feel in control. When anxiety creeps in, even the simplest tasks can feel overwhelming, and the pressure becomes almost unbearable. But the good news is that there are ways to handle stress like a pro, and by understanding what triggers your anxiety and how to manage it, you can start feeling more empowered in your daily life.

This chapter will take you through why pressure can feel so intense for teens with PDA, practical quick-relief tactics to reduce stress in the moment, and long-term strategies to help manage anxiety more effectively over time. Learning how to handle pressure is not about eliminating stress completely—that's impossible for anyone—but it's about learning how to manage it in ways that keep it from controlling your life.

By understanding your relationship with pressure and finding methods that work for you, you'll be better equipped to navigate the challenges of being a PDA teen. Let's explore why pressure feels so intense and what you can do about it.

## Why the Pressure Feels So Intense

For teens with PDA, pressure and demands can feel ten times more overwhelming than they do for others. This is because of the unique way your brain processes stress and how it reacts to everyday demands. PDA is rooted in an anxiety-driven need to avoid demands, so when you're faced with pressure, your brain may interpret it as a threat, even if the demand seems small or reasonable. Understanding why the pressure feels so intense is the first step toward learning how to manage it.

The fight, flight, or freeze response is at the core of how PDA teens react to pressure. This response is an automatic reaction to stress and is designed to protect you from perceived threats. When your brain feels overwhelmed by a demand—whether it's homework, a social event, or even getting out of bed in the morning—it might trigger one of these responses. You might feel like running away from the task (flight), arguing or refusing to do it (fight), or completely shutting down and not being able to respond (freeze).

This heightened response to pressure makes it difficult to handle demands in the same way others do. While some people might feel a bit stressed about a big assignment or a social obligation, teens with PDA often experience a full-blown anxiety response. This can make even small tasks feel like mountains that are impossible to climb. It's not about being lazy or unmotivated—it's about your brain's reaction to stress.

Another reason pressure feels so intense for teens with PDA is that you may feel like you have little control over your environment. When demands are placed on you without your input or when expectations feel rigid, the anxiety can skyrocket. The need to feel in control is a common theme for people with PDA, and when that control is taken away, the pressure can feel unbearable.

It's also important to recognize that stress builds up over time. Even if a single demand doesn't seem like a big deal, when multiple demands pile up—like schoolwork, family responsibilities, and social obligations—the pressure can quickly become overwhelming. This cumulative effect can leave you feeling trapped and unable to cope.

Understanding why pressure feels so intense can help you be more compassionate with yourself. It's not a weakness or failure on your part—it's the way your brain is wired to respond to stress. In the next section, we'll explore quick stress-relief tactics that can help you reduce pressure in the moment when it feels like too much to handle.

# Quick Stress-Relief Tactics That Really Work

When the pressure feels like it's mounting and you're on the verge of a meltdown, having quick stress-relief tactics can be a lifesaver. These are strategies you can use in the moment to calm your mind, reduce anxiety, and regain a sense of control. While they won't eliminate the underlying causes of stress, they can help you manage the immediate pressure and prevent it from spiraling into something more overwhelming.

One of the most effective quick-relief tactics is **deep breathing**. When you're feeling anxious, your breathing becomes shallow and rapid, which only increases your feelings of stress. By taking slow, deep breaths, you can send a signal to your brain that it's okay to relax. Try the 4-7-8 method: inhale deeply for 4 seconds, hold your breath for 7 seconds, and then exhale slowly for 8 seconds. Repeat this a few times, and you'll start to notice your heart rate slowing and your body relaxing.

Another useful tactic is **grounding exercises**. When anxiety starts to take over, grounding techniques can help bring you back to the present moment and away from the overwhelming thoughts in your mind. One simple grounding exercise is the "5-4-3-2-1" method: identify 5 things you can see around you, 4 things you can touch, 3 things you can hear, 2 things you can smell, and 1 thing you can taste. Focusing on your senses helps distract your mind from the pressure and reduces anxiety.

**Physical movement** is another quick way to relieve stress. When you're feeling anxious, your body can become tense and rigid, which only adds to the feeling of pressure. A short walk, a few minutes of stretching, or even a quick dance break can help release tension and get your blood flowing. Movement also helps release endorphins, the brain's natural feel-good chemicals, which can improve your mood and reduce stress.

If you're in a situation where you can't physically move, **visualization** can be a powerful tool. Close your eyes and imagine a place where you feel calm and safe—whether it's a beach, a forest, or a cozy room. Picture yourself in that place, focusing on the sights, sounds, and feelings associated with it. Visualization helps transport your mind to a peaceful setting, even if just for a few minutes, which can help reduce anxiety in the moment.

Finally, **distraction** can be a helpful quick-relief tactic when the pressure feels too intense. Engaging in a calming activity that takes your mind off the stress—like reading, drawing, or listening to music—can help you reset. The key is to find something that fully absorbs your attention so that your mind gets a break from the overwhelming thoughts and feelings.

These quick-relief tactics are not meant to solve the deeper issues behind your stress, but they can help you get through the toughest moments. In the next section, we'll explore long-term strategies for managing anxiety, so you can handle pressure more effectively over time.

# Long-Term Strategies for Managing Anxiety

While quick-relief tactics are great for managing stress in the moment, it's important to have long-term strategies in place to reduce anxiety and prevent it from building up. Long-term anxiety management is about creating a lifestyle that supports your mental health and helps you navigate the challenges of PDA with more resilience. These strategies take time and effort, but they can make a significant difference in how you handle pressure in the long run.

One of the most important long-term strategies is **establishing a routine**. Routines provide structure and predictability, which can help reduce anxiety. When you know what to expect each day, the demands of life feel more manageable. Create a daily routine that includes time for schoolwork, relaxation, physical activity, and hobbies. Having a consistent routine can help you feel more in control of your time and reduce the stress of unpredictable demands.

**Mindfulness and meditation** are also powerful tools for managing anxiety over the long term. Mindfulness involves being present in the moment without judgment, which can help you become more aware of your thoughts and feelings without becoming overwhelmed by them. Regular meditation practice can help calm your mind, improve your focus, and reduce anxiety. Start with just a few minutes a day, using guided meditation apps or mindfulness exercises, and gradually build up your practice.

**Cognitive-behavioral strategies** (CBT) can also be incredibly helpful for managing anxiety. CBT involves identifying negative thought patterns that contribute to anxiety and replacing them with more balanced, realistic thoughts. For example, if you're feeling anxious about an upcoming test, you might have thoughts like, "I'm going to fail," or "I'll never get through this." CBT encourages you to challenge these thoughts by asking yourself, "Is this really true?" or "What's the worst that could happen?" Over time, CBT can help you develop healthier thought patterns and reduce the intensity of your anxiety.

**Physical health** plays a big role in managing anxiety, too. Regular exercise, a balanced diet, and adequate sleep are essential for maintaining mental and emotional well-being. Exercise helps reduce stress hormones and releases endorphins, which improve your mood. Eating a healthy diet can stabilize your energy levels and mood, while getting enough sleep is crucial for reducing irritability and stress. Taking care of your physical health can have a positive impact on your ability to handle pressure.

Finally, building a **support system** is a key long-term strategy for managing anxiety. Having people you can talk to—whether it's friends, family, or a therapist—can provide emotional support when you're feeling overwhelmed. Surround yourself with people who understand your challenges and are willing to listen without judgment. Knowing that you have a network of support can help you feel less isolated and more capable of managing stress.

Long-term anxiety management is about making choices that support your mental health on a daily basis. By incorporating these strategies into your life, you can build resilience and reduce the impact of stress, making it easier to handle pressure when it arises.

# Chapter 8

# Building Confidence and Resilience

Living with Pathological Demand Avoidance (PDA) as a teen can sometimes make it feel like you're constantly fighting an uphill battle. Between school pressures, family expectations, and social interactions, it can be difficult to feel confident and capable. However, building confidence and resilience is not only possible—it's essential. Confidence allows you to trust in your abilities, while resilience helps you bounce back from the challenges you face. Together, these qualities will empower you to navigate life with PDA more effectively.

Confidence and resilience aren't traits you're born with—they're skills that can be developed over time. They're built through small victories, learning from setbacks, and finding strength in your unique experiences. This chapter will guide you through discovering your personal strengths as a teen with PDA, how to build confidence even on tough days, and strategies for bouncing back from setbacks and challenges. By focusing on your growth, you'll start to see that you're more capable than you might realize.

Let's start by exploring how you can find your inner strength, even when living with PDA feels like a constant struggle. From there, we'll move on to practical steps for building confidence and resilience, so you can face life's challenges with more determination and self-belief.

## Finding Your Strength in PDA

For many teens with PDA, it's easy to focus on the difficulties and challenges you face each day. The anxiety that comes with demands, the avoidance behaviors, and the pressure to meet expectations can sometimes overshadow the fact that you have unique strengths. However, finding your strength in PDA means recognizing that you are not defined by your struggles—you are defined by how you rise above them.

One of the first steps in finding your strength is shifting your perspective on what it means to live with PDA. Instead of viewing PDA solely as a challenge, try to see it as part of what makes you who you are. Living with PDA has likely taught you valuable lessons about yourself and the world around you. For example, you've learned how to navigate overwhelming situations, communicate your needs, and manage your anxiety. These skills are strengths, even if they don't always feel that way.

Another important aspect of finding your strength is recognizing the moments when you've overcome obstacles. It's easy to downplay your achievements, especially when you're comparing yourself to others. But every time you've faced a challenge—whether it's completing a homework assignment, attending a social event, or standing up for yourself—you've demonstrated resilience. Celebrate these small victories, because they're proof that you're stronger than you think.

In addition to your personal strengths, living with PDA can give you a unique perspective on the world. You may have a heightened sense of empathy because you understand what it's like to struggle. You may be highly creative, finding innovative solutions to avoid demands or manage your anxiety. These are strengths that not everyone has, and they're part of what makes you unique.

It's also helpful to focus on your passions and interests. What are the things that light you up? Whether it's art, music, sports, or technology, engaging in activities you love can help you feel more confident in your abilities. When you're doing something you're passionate about, the pressure often fades, and you're able to focus on your strengths rather than your challenges.

Finally, finding your strength in PDA means acknowledging that you're still growing. You don't have to have everything figured out right now. Every day is an opportunity to learn more about yourself and how you can navigate the world. Embrace the journey, and remember that your strength lies not in being perfect, but in your ability to keep going, even when things are tough.

## How to Build Confidence, Even on Tough Days

Building confidence can feel like an impossible task, especially on days when the anxiety and pressure of PDA seem overwhelming. But confidence isn't about feeling strong all the time—it's about learning to trust yourself and your abilities, even when things feel difficult. The good news is that confidence can be built, and with time, you'll start to believe in your own capabilities, even on the toughest days.

The first step in building confidence is **setting small, achievable goals**. When you set goals that are realistic and within reach, you give yourself the opportunity to succeed. Each time you meet a goal, no matter how small, your confidence will grow. For example, if you're struggling with homework, set a goal to complete just one section of the assignment. Once you've achieved that, set another small goal. Over time, these small wins add up, and your confidence will increase as you see that you're capable of meeting challenges head-on.

Another important part of building confidence is **celebrating your successes**. It's easy to overlook your achievements, especially if they don't seem as significant as what others are doing. But your journey is unique, and every success—whether it's completing a task, managing your anxiety, or communicating your needs—is worth celebrating. Take the time to acknowledge your progress, and don't be afraid to give yourself credit for the hard work you're doing.

On tough days, it's also helpful to practice **positive self-talk**. The way you talk to yourself has a powerful impact on your confidence. When you're feeling down, it's easy to fall into negative thought patterns like, "I'm not good enough" or "I can't do this." But these thoughts aren't based in reality—they're a reflection of your anxiety. To build confidence, practice replacing these negative thoughts with more balanced ones. For example, instead of thinking, "I'll never be able to do this," try saying, "This is hard, but I've faced hard things before and gotten through them."

Building confidence also involves **stepping outside of your comfort zone**—even if it's just a little bit at a time. When you challenge yourself to try new things or face situations that make you anxious, you build resilience and prove to yourself that you're capable of more than you might think. This doesn't mean you have to take huge risks all at once. Start with small challenges, like speaking up in class or trying a new hobby, and gradually build from there.

It's also important to **surround yourself with supportive people** who believe in you. Confidence isn't something you have to build on your own—having friends, family, or mentors who encourage you can make a big difference. When you're feeling uncertain, lean on the people who remind you of your strengths and help you see the progress you've made.

Finally, remember that building confidence is a process. There will be days when you feel strong and capable, and there will be days when your confidence wavers. That's okay. What matters is that you keep showing up for yourself and keep taking steps forward, even when it's hard. Confidence isn't about being perfect—it's about trusting in your ability to grow and learn.

## Bouncing Back from Setbacks and Challenges

Setbacks and challenges are a normal part of life, but for teens with PDA, they can feel particularly discouraging. When things don't go as planned or when you face a difficult situation, it's easy to feel like giving up. However, resilience—the ability to bounce back from setbacks—is a skill that you can develop. Building resilience will help you face challenges with more determination and confidence, knowing that you have the strength to overcome them.

The first step in building resilience is **acknowledging that setbacks are part of life**. No one is perfect, and everyone experiences challenges along the way. It's important to recognize that setbacks don't define you—they're simply moments of difficulty that you can learn from. When you face a setback, instead of seeing it as a failure, try to view it as an opportunity for growth. Ask yourself, "What can I learn from this experience? How can I use this challenge to become stronger?"

Another important part of resilience is **practicing self-compassion**. When you face a setback, it's easy to be hard on yourself or feel like you've let yourself or others down. But being kind to yourself during difficult times is essential for building resilience. Instead of criticizing yourself for what went wrong, practice self-compassion by acknowledging your feelings and reminding yourself that it's okay to make mistakes. Treat yourself with the same kindness and understanding that you would offer to a friend in the same situation.

Resilience also involves **problem-solving**. When you face a challenge, it's helpful to break the problem down into smaller, more manageable steps. Ask yourself,

"What's one thing I can do to start moving forward?" By focusing on small, actionable steps, you can begin to regain a sense of control and make progress, even when the situation feels overwhelming. Problem-solving not only helps you overcome setbacks, but it also builds your confidence in your ability to handle future challenges.

**Maintaining a positive outlook** is another key aspect of resilience. This doesn't mean ignoring the difficulties you're facing—it means choosing to focus on what you can control and believing in your ability to get through tough times. When you're in the middle of a setback, it's easy to feel like things will never get better. But resilience involves trusting that, with time and effort, you'll find a way forward. Try to focus on the bigger picture and remind yourself that setbacks are temporary.

Building resilience also involves **seeking support when you need it**. You don't have to face challenges alone. Whether it's talking to a friend, a family member, or a counselor, reaching out for support can make a big difference in how you handle setbacks. Sometimes, just having someone to listen and offer encouragement can help you see the situation from a new perspective and give you the strength to keep going.

Finally, remember that resilience is built over time. Every time you face a challenge and find a way to move forward, you're strengthening your ability to bounce back. The more you practice resilience, the more confident you'll become in your ability to handle whatever life throws your way. Resilience doesn't mean you won't face difficulties—it means that, no matter what happens, you have the strength to keep going.

# Chapter 9

# The Road to Independence – Making Decisions That Work for You

As a teen with Pathological Demand Avoidance (PDA), the idea of making independent decisions can feel both empowering and overwhelming. The thought of shaping your future and making choices that align with who you are can be exciting, but when the pressure builds up, it can also trigger feelings of anxiety. Independence is a journey, and it's about learning how to navigate decision-making in a way that feels manageable and, most importantly, true to who you are.

The road to independence is different for everyone, but for teens with PDA, it often involves finding ways to make decisions that don't feel overwhelming. Independence isn't just about taking on more responsibilities—it's about making choices that align with your strengths, values, and aspirations while managing the anxiety that comes with it. Whether you're deciding on your next steps in life, solving everyday problems, or planning for the future, learning how to make decisions that work for you is key to building the independence you deserve.

We'll explore what it means to make choices that feel right for your future, how to develop problem-solving skills in a way that works with your PDA, and how to create a future that genuinely excites you. Independence doesn't have to mean doing everything perfectly—it's about discovering what works for you, even when things feel uncertain.

## Making Choices That Feel Right for Your Future

The idea of making choices about your future can feel intimidating, especially when it seems like everyone around you has a plan, and you're still figuring things out. But it's important to remember that your journey doesn't have to look like anyone else's. Making choices that feel right for your future is about tuning into what matters most to you, rather than trying to meet the expectations of others.

One of the first steps in making choices that align with your future is recognizing your own values and interests. What are the things that truly excite you? What activities or subjects make you feel alive and engaged? These are the areas where your strengths lie, and they can serve as important clues for what direction you might want to take in the future. Whether it's a passion for art, technology, animals, or social causes, following your interests can help guide you toward choices that feel fulfilling.

It's also important to understand that making choices for your future doesn't have to be a one-time, all-or-nothing decision. You don't have to know exactly what you want to do with your life right now, and it's okay if your path changes over time. Making smaller decisions that feel right in the moment can help you build confidence in your ability to shape your future. For example, instead of stressing about what career to choose, focus on what classes or activities you enjoy right now and see where that leads.

When making choices, it's also essential to consider how demands and expectations might affect your anxiety. For teens with PDA, the pressure to make "the right choice" can feel paralyzing. To combat this, try breaking down big decisions into smaller, more manageable steps. Instead of thinking, "I need to figure out my entire future," ask yourself, "What's one small choice I can make today that feels right?" By taking it one step at a time, you can reduce the overwhelm and make decisions that work for you.

Another important aspect of making choices for your future is learning how to balance your own needs with the expectations of others. Parents, teachers, and friends may have opinions about what they think you should do, but ultimately, the decisions you make should reflect your values and what feels right for you. It's okay to seek advice and guidance from others, but remember that your future is yours to shape.

Finally, building independence means trusting yourself and your ability to make decisions. It's normal to feel uncertain or anxious about the future, but learning to listen to your intuition and trust your instincts will help you make choices that align with who you are. Independence is about taking control of your own path, even when it feels a little scary. By making decisions that feel right for your future, you're setting the stage for a life that reflects your true self.

## Developing Problem-Solving Skills, PDA Style

Problem-solving is a key part of building independence, but for teens with PDA, the process of solving problems can feel particularly challenging. The anxiety that comes with facing a demand or pressure can make it hard to think clearly and come up with solutions. However, problem-solving is a skill that can be developed, and by finding strategies that work with your PDA, you can learn to tackle challenges in a way that feels more manageable.

One of the first steps in developing problem-solving skills is understanding your own problem-solving style. Everyone approaches problems differently, and for teens with PDA, the need for control and avoidance of demands can influence how you react to challenges. You might find that you tend to avoid problems altogether or feel overwhelmed by the pressure to find a solution. Recognizing these patterns is the first step toward developing a problem-solving style that works for you.

A helpful approach to problem-solving is breaking the problem down into smaller, more manageable parts. When you're faced with a big challenge, it can feel overwhelming to try and solve the whole thing at once. Instead, break the problem down into smaller steps and tackle each one individually. For example, if you're struggling with a school project, start by breaking it down into tasks like researching, outlining, and drafting. By focusing on one step at a time, the problem feels less overwhelming, and you can make progress without feeling paralyzed by the pressure.

Another important aspect of problem-solving is giving yourself time and space to process the problem. For teens with PDA, the pressure to come up with a solution right away can trigger anxiety and avoidance. Instead of forcing yourself to solve the problem immediately, give yourself permission to take a break and come back to it with a clearer mind. This might involve taking a walk, practicing mindfulness, or engaging in a calming activity that helps you relax. When you're feeling more grounded, it's easier to approach the problem with a fresh perspective.

Creative problem-solving is another valuable skill for teens with PDA. Because you're used to finding ways to avoid demands, you might already have a natural ability to think outside the box. Use this creativity to your advantage when solving problems. Instead of sticking to traditional solutions, think about how you can approach the problem from a different angle. For example, if a school assignment feels overwhelming, could you propose an alternative project that better suits your interests? By embracing your creativity, you can find solutions that work for you.

Finally, don't be afraid to ask for help when solving problems. Independence doesn't mean you have to do everything on your own. Sometimes, the best way to solve a problem is by seeking advice or support from others. Whether it's a friend, family member, or teacher, reaching out for help can provide new insights and help you feel less isolated in your problem-solving process.

By developing problem-solving skills that work with your PDA, you'll be better equipped to handle challenges as they arise. Problem-solving is a key part of independence, and with practice, you'll learn to approach problems with more confidence and creativity.

## Creating a Future You're Excited About

The future can feel uncertain and even scary at times, especially when the pressures of PDA make it hard to navigate decisions and expectations. But creating a future you're excited about is possible, and it starts with envisioning a life that reflects your true self. Independence isn't just about making decisions—it's about creating a path that feels authentic and meaningful to you.

One of the first steps in creating a future you're excited about is allowing yourself to dream. It's easy to get caught up in the practicalities of life and focus on what's expected of you, but building a future that excites you means tuning into your passions and aspirations. What are the things that light you up? What dreams do you have for yourself, even if they seem far off or unrealistic right now? Allow yourself to explore these ideas without judgment, knowing that your future is yours to shape.

Once you've connected with your passions, it's time to start thinking about how you can bring those dreams to life. This doesn't mean you have to have everything figured out right away—instead, focus on taking small steps toward the things that excite you. For example, if you're passionate about animals, could you start volunteering at a local shelter or explore courses related to animal care? By taking small steps toward your goals, you can start building a future that feels aligned with your interests and values.

Another important part of creating a future you're excited about is staying open to change. Your path might not look exactly how you expect it to, and that's okay. As you grow and learn more about yourself, your interests and goals may shift. Embrace the uncertainty and allow yourself to adapt as you discover new opportunities. Independence is about being flexible and trusting that, no matter what changes, you're capable of creating a fulfilling future.

It's also important to focus on the process rather than the destination. Building a future you're excited about isn't just about achieving a specific goal—it's about enjoying the journey and finding meaning in the steps you take along the way. Whether it's learning new skills, exploring new passions, or building meaningful relationships, each experience contributes to the life you're creating. Celebrate the progress you make, no matter how small, and trust that you're moving in the right direction.

Finally, creating a future you're excited about means letting go of the pressure to meet other people's expectations. Your future doesn't have to look like anyone else's, and it's okay if your path is different from what others expect. Focus on what feels right for you, and remember that your independence is about building a life that reflects who you are, not who others want you to be.

By taking ownership of your choices, developing problem-solving skills, and staying true to your passions, you can create a future that excites you and brings out the best in who you are. Independence isn't about having everything figured out—it's about embracing the journey and trusting in your ability to create a meaningful and fulfilling life.

# Chapter 10

# Redefining Identity – Who Are You?

As a teenager, you're probably already thinking about who you are and what defines you. For teens with Pathological Demand Avoidance (PDA), this question can be even more complex. Identity is shaped by so many factors—your experiences, interests, relationships, and the way you navigate the world around you. Living with PDA adds an additional layer of uniqueness to your journey of self-discovery. You might feel like you don't fit into the mold others expect you to, and that's okay. In fact, one of the most empowering things you can do is redefine what identity means for you on your own terms.

This chapter is about exploring who you are beyond the labels and expectations placed on you. It's about embracing your true self, celebrating the things that make you unique, and moving beyond the stereotypes that may have been imposed on you because of PDA.

Identity is not something fixed—it's something that evolves as you grow and learn more about yourself. By redefining your identity in a way that reflects your true self, you'll find a deeper sense of confidence and acceptance.

We'll start by looking at how PDA influences your sense of identity, how you can embrace who you are fully, and why it's important to challenge the labels and stereotypes that might limit your potential.

## PDA, Identity, and Finding Your True Self

Living with PDA can sometimes feel like it defines you, especially when it shapes so many of your experiences. You might feel that PDA limits your ability to fit in or meet the expectations others have of you. But PDA is just one part of who you are—it's not the whole picture. Finding your true self means exploring all the different facets of your identity, beyond the diagnosis.

Your true self is made up of your values, passions, strengths, and even your challenges. It's easy to get caught up in thinking about the things you struggle with because of PDA, but it's just as important to acknowledge your unique strengths. For example, many teens with PDA are incredibly creative, empathetic, and resourceful. These are qualities that help shape your identity in powerful and positive ways.

Another part of finding your true self is recognizing that identity is not something that has to be figured out all at once. It's okay if you're still discovering who you are. Your identity will continue to evolve as you have new experiences, try new things, and learn more about what matters to you. Give yourself the freedom to explore different aspects of your personality and interests, without feeling pressured to fit into a specific category.

One of the challenges of living with PDA is that you might feel like the way you respond to the world is different from others. This can sometimes make it hard to figure out where you fit in. But your differences are part of what makes you unique, and they can be a source of strength once you begin to accept and embrace them. Instead of seeing PDA as something that limits you, try to think of it as part of the tapestry of your identity. It's one piece of the puzzle, but it doesn't define the entire picture.

To find your true self, it's also important to reflect on what brings you joy and fulfillment. What activities make you feel most like yourself? What kind of environment helps you thrive? These are questions that can help guide you in understanding who you are. Your true self isn't determined by what others expect of you—it's shaped by what resonates with you on a deeper level.

## How to Embrace Who You Are and Celebrate It

Embracing who you are, especially when you feel different from others, can be challenging. However, learning to accept and celebrate yourself is one of the most empowering things you can do. It allows you to step into your true identity with confidence and pride, knowing that who you are is valuable, just as you are.

One of the first steps in embracing who you are is practicing self-compassion. Living with PDA might mean that you face certain challenges that others don't, and it's easy to be hard on yourself when things feel difficult. But self-compassion means recognizing that everyone has struggles, and that you deserve kindness and understanding, especially from yourself. Instead of focusing on what you think you "should" be able to do, focus on what you've already accomplished. Celebrate your strengths and the unique qualities that make you who you are.

It's also important to stop comparing yourself to others. In today's world, especially with social media, it can feel like everyone else has it all figured out. But remember that everyone's journey is different, and comparing yourself to others only distracts you from your own path. Embracing who you are means recognizing that your journey is yours to navigate, and that your experiences are valuable in their own right.

Another key to embracing yourself is letting go of perfectionism. It's easy to feel like you need to live up to certain expectations, whether they come from your family, friends, or society at large. But striving for perfection can be exhausting and ultimately unfulfilling. Instead, focus on being authentic. The more you allow yourself to be real—flaws and all—the more you'll begin to feel at home in your own skin. You don't have to be perfect to be worthy of love and acceptance.

Celebrating yourself also means recognizing your achievements, no matter how small they may seem. Whether it's managing a challenging situation, completing a task, or simply getting through a tough day, take the time to acknowledge your efforts. These moments of celebration help reinforce the idea that you are capable, resilient, and deserving of recognition.

It's also helpful to surround yourself with people who appreciate you for who you are. When you have friends, family, or mentors who see your worth and encourage you to be your authentic self, it becomes easier to embrace and celebrate yourself. These supportive relationships serve as a reminder that you don't have to change who you are to fit in—you are already enough, just as you are.

## Redefining Labels: Moving Beyond Stereotypes

Living with PDA often means that others may try to label you in ways that don't fully capture who you are. You might be labeled as "difficult," "stubborn," or "uncooperative" because of your avoidance behaviors. These labels can be limiting and hurtful, and they don't reflect the full complexity of who you are as a person. But the good news is that you have the power to redefine these labels and move beyond the stereotypes that may have been placed on you.

The first step in moving beyond labels is recognizing that they don't define you. Just because someone has called you "difficult" doesn't mean that's who you are.

Often, these labels are a reflection of other people's misunderstandings of PDA, rather than an accurate representation of your true self. By letting go of these labels, you free yourself from the expectations that others have placed on you and allow yourself to step into your own identity.

Another way to move beyond stereotypes is by challenging them. If someone calls you "lazy" because you avoid certain demands, take a moment to reflect on why you avoid those tasks. Is it because you're truly lazy, or is it because those tasks trigger anxiety and overwhelm? By understanding the reasons behind your behaviors, you can begin to challenge the labels that don't serve you. You can also educate others about PDA, helping them see that avoidance isn't about laziness or defiance—it's about managing anxiety in a way that feels safe for you.

It's also important to create your own labels that feel empowering. Instead of allowing others to define you, think about how you want to define yourself. For example, if someone calls you "uncooperative," you might choose to redefine yourself as "independent" or "creative," recognizing that your need to do things in your own way is a strength. By choosing empowering labels, you take control of your identity and move beyond the limiting stereotypes that others might impose on you.

Another key to moving beyond stereotypes is surrounding yourself with people who see the real you. When you're constantly around people who misunderstand you or label you negatively, it can be hard to break free from those stereotypes. But when you have friends and family who see your strengths and encourage you to be your authentic self, it becomes easier to redefine your identity in a way that feels true to you.

Finally, moving beyond labels means embracing the idea that identity is fluid. You don't have to fit into a specific box, and you don't have to be the same person tomorrow that you are today. As you grow and learn more about yourself, your identity will continue to evolve. By staying open to this process, you give yourself the freedom to redefine who you are on your own terms, without being limited by the labels others place on you.

By redefining labels and moving beyond stereotypes, you empower yourself to live more authentically and confidently. Your identity is yours to shape, and by embracing who you are, you'll find a deeper sense of fulfillment and acceptance.

# Chapter 11

# Managing the Chaos – Demands, Overwhelm, and PDA

Living with Pathological Demand Avoidance (PDA) often feels like you're stuck in a constant tug-of-war between demands and the overwhelming pressure they create. From simple requests like getting dressed in the morning to larger responsibilities such as school assignments or social commitments, demands can seem to loom over you, triggering anxiety and avoidance. For teens with PDA, the chaos of daily life can feel like an endless series of battles, but it doesn't have to be that way. Understanding why demands feel so intense, and learning how to manage the overwhelm they create, is key to reclaiming control over your life.

This chapter will break down why demands can feel so intense for those with PDA and provide you with tools for managing the overwhelm in your everyday life. It's not about trying to eliminate demands entirely—that's unrealistic—but about finding strategies that allow you to navigate them in a way that feels less stressful and more empowering. Finally, we'll explore how you can reclaim your power over external pressures, so you can approach life with more confidence and less anxiety.

Let's start by understanding why demands have such a strong impact on teens with PDA and how that knowledge can help you manage the chaos they create.

## Why Demands Feel So Intense: Breaking It Down

For most people, daily demands are just a normal part of life—they get up, go to school or work, complete tasks, and move on. But for teens with PDA, even the smallest demands can trigger an overwhelming sense of anxiety and avoidance. Understanding why this happens can help you manage the intensity of these feelings and reduce the stress they create.

One of the main reasons demands feel so intense for teens with PDA is because they trigger the brain's **fight, flight, or freeze** response. This response is your body's natural reaction to a perceived threat, and for people with PDA, demands are often interpreted as threats. When someone asks you to do something, no matter how small, your brain may react as though you're facing something dangerous, leading to feelings of panic or a strong desire to avoid the task altogether.

Another reason demands feel so overwhelming is because they can represent a loss of control. For teens with PDA, having control over your environment and decisions is crucial to feeling safe and comfortable. When someone places a demand on you—whether it's a teacher assigning homework or a parent asking you to clean your room—it can feel like that control is being taken away. This loss of control can lead to resistance, as your brain tries to regain a sense of autonomy.

The unpredictability of demands also plays a role in why they feel so intense. If you're unsure of what's going to be asked of you or when it's going to happen, it can create a constant state of anxiety. The anticipation of a demand can be just as stressful as the demand itself, leaving you feeling on edge even when no immediate tasks are being presented.

It's also important to recognize that demands can build up over time. When you're already feeling overwhelmed, even a small request can feel like the final straw that sends everything spiraling out of control. This is known as the **cumulative effect**—when multiple demands pile up, they become increasingly difficult to manage, leading to a sense of total overwhelm.

Finally, the intensity of demands for teens with PDA is often tied to a fear of failure. You might worry that you won't be able to meet the expectations placed on you, leading to anxiety about the outcome. This fear can make even simple tasks feel impossible because the pressure to succeed becomes so great that avoidance feels like the only option.

Understanding why demands feel so intense is the first step toward managing them more effectively. In the next section, we'll explore practical tools for reducing overwhelm in your everyday life, so you can start to feel more in control.

## Tools for Managing Overwhelm in Everyday Life

When demands and the pressure they create start to feel overwhelming, having practical tools in your toolkit can make all the difference. Managing overwhelm isn't about eliminating demands entirely—it's about finding strategies that help you navigate them in a way that feels less stressful. The goal is to reduce the intensity of the demands you face and give yourself the space to manage them without feeling completely overwhelmed.

One of the most effective tools for managing overwhelm is **breaking tasks down into smaller steps**. When you're faced with a large task, like a school project or a chore at home, it can feel impossible to tackle the whole thing at once. Instead of trying to complete the entire task in one go, break it down into smaller, more manageable parts. For example, if you're working on an essay, start by brainstorming ideas, then move on to creating an outline, and finally write the introduction. By focusing on one small step at a time, the task feels less daunting, and you can make steady progress without becoming overwhelmed.

Another helpful tool is **creating a routine** that provides structure to your day. Routines help reduce the unpredictability of demands by giving you a clear plan for how your day will unfold. If you know when you're going to do certain tasks—like schoolwork, chores, or relaxation—it becomes easier to manage your time and avoid the anxiety that comes with unexpected demands. Your routine doesn't have to be rigid, but having a general outline of your day can help create a sense of control and reduce feelings of chaos.

**Setting boundaries** is also essential for managing overwhelm. For teens with PDA, it's important to recognize when you're reaching your limit and need to say no to additional demands. This might mean telling a friend that you need some time to yourself or letting your parents know that you'll get to a task later when you're feeling more capable. Setting boundaries helps protect your mental and emotional energy, so you're not constantly running on empty.

**Mindfulness techniques** can also be incredibly effective in managing overwhelm. When anxiety starts to build, practicing mindfulness can help ground you in the present moment and reduce the intensity of your emotions. Simple mindfulness exercises, like focusing on your breathing or engaging in a short meditation, can help calm your mind and body, giving you the space to approach demands with more clarity and less stress.

It's also helpful to **build in regular breaks** throughout your day. When you're faced with a series of demands, it's easy to feel like you need to power through and get everything done at once. But taking regular breaks is important for maintaining your energy and preventing burnout. Whether it's a short walk, a few minutes of stretching, or simply sitting in silence for a few moments, breaks allow your brain to reset and recharge, making it easier to tackle the next task.

Finally, **asking for help** is a crucial tool for managing overwhelm. Independence doesn't mean you have to do everything on your own, and reaching out for support when you need it is a sign of strength, not weakness. Whether it's asking a friend to help you with a project or talking to a family member about how you're feeling, seeking support can provide relief and make it easier to manage the demands in your life.

## Reclaiming Your Power Over External Pressures

For teens with PDA, it's common to feel like external pressures—whether they come from school, family, or society—are constantly weighing down on you. These pressures can make it feel like you're not in control of your own life, leading to feelings of frustration and helplessness. However, you have the ability to reclaim your power over these external pressures and approach life's demands with more confidence and resilience.

One of the first steps in reclaiming your power is **changing your perspective on demands**. Instead of seeing every demand as something negative or threatening, try to reframe it as an opportunity to take control of the situation. For example, if you're asked to complete a task that feels overwhelming, remind yourself that you have the power to choose how and when you approach it. This might involve negotiating with others to find a compromise that works for you, or breaking the task down into smaller steps, as mentioned earlier. By shifting your mindset, you can start to see demands as challenges you can navigate, rather than obstacles that stand in your way.

Another important aspect of reclaiming your power is **asserting your boundaries**. External pressures often feel overwhelming because it seems like others are dictating your actions. But setting boundaries allows you to take back control of your time and energy. This might mean saying no to certain social commitments, asking for more time to complete an assignment, or letting others know that you need space to recharge. Boundaries give you the freedom to manage demands in a way that feels comfortable for you, without feeling like you're constantly being pulled in different directions.

**Self-advocacy** is another key to reclaiming your power over external pressures. Self-advocacy means speaking up for yourself and communicating your needs to others in a clear and confident way. This could involve explaining to your teachers how PDA affects your ability to meet deadlines or telling your parents what kind of support you need at home. By advocating for yourself, you're taking control of the situation and ensuring that your needs are being considered.

It's also helpful to **focus on what you can control**. There will always be external pressures that you can't completely eliminate, but by focusing on the things you can control—like how you respond to demands or how you manage your time—you'll start to feel more empowered. Instead of getting caught up in what others expect of you, shift your attention to what you can do to make the situation more manageable for yourself. This might mean creating a personalized plan for how to tackle a task or setting aside time each day to focus on self-care.

Finally, reclaiming your power means **celebrating your progress**. It's easy to focus on the demands you haven't met or the tasks that still feel overwhelming, but it's important to acknowledge the progress you've made. Each time you successfully navigate a demand or manage a difficult situation, you're building resilience and proving to yourself that you're capable of handling external pressures. Celebrate these victories, no matter how small they may seem, and use them as a reminder of your strength.

By reclaiming your power over external pressures, you'll start to feel more in control of your life and more confident in your ability to handle demands. Demands and expectations may always be a part of life, but by taking ownership of how you respond to them, you can reduce the chaos and approach challenges with more confidence and resilience.

# Chapter 12

# Technology and PDA – Balancing the Digital World

Technology plays a huge role in the lives of most teenagers today. From smartphones to laptops, social media to streaming platforms, the digital world has become an integral part of everyday life. For teens with Pathological Demand Avoidance (PDA), technology can offer a safe and enjoyable space to escape from the pressures of the outside world. However, it can also contribute to feelings of overwhelm, especially when it becomes difficult to disconnect or balance screen time with real-life responsibilities.

This chapter will discuss the relationship between PDA and technology, how to create a healthy balance between the digital and real worlds, and how to navigate social media without feeling overloaded. Technology is neither all good nor all bad—it's about finding a way to engage with it in a way that works for you. With the right strategies, you can enjoy the benefits of technology without letting it take over your life or add to your anxiety.

Let's start by examining how PDA teens tend to interact with technology and the unique challenges and opportunities it presents.

## The PDA Relationship with Tech and Screen Time

For teens with PDA, technology can feel like both a sanctuary and a potential source of stress. On one hand, the digital world offers a space where you can avoid the demands of real life. You can escape into video games, social media, or streaming platforms without the immediate pressure of in-person demands. Technology provides a sense of control that's often hard to find in the real world—online, you can choose when to engage and when to disconnect, and you can avoid overwhelming social interactions if you need to.

However, this relationship with technology can also have its downsides. For some PDA teens, screen time can quickly spiral out of control, becoming a way to avoid real-life responsibilities like schoolwork, chores, or social commitments. While it's natural to want to escape into the digital world when things feel overwhelming, relying too heavily on technology as a coping mechanism can lead to more anxiety in the long run. The more you avoid real-life demands, the bigger those demands feel, and eventually, they become even harder to face.

Another challenge with technology is the **constant availability** of digital distractions. Social media notifications, new episodes of your favorite show, and endless streams of content can make it difficult to step away. For teens with PDA, the need for control can lead to an almost compulsive need to check notifications or engage with content, creating a cycle of dependency that's hard to break. This can lead to feelings of guilt or frustration when you know you should be focusing on other tasks but can't seem to pull yourself away from your screen.

Additionally, technology can contribute to **sensory overload**, which is already a challenge for many PDA teens. Bright screens, constant notifications, and the fast pace of online interactions can leave you feeling mentally and physically drained. This sensory input can make it difficult to relax or focus on other activities, leading to a sense of overwhelm that spills over into your offline life.

Despite these challenges, technology doesn't have to be something negative. It's all about finding a balance that allows you to enjoy the benefits of the digital world without letting it control your life. In the next section, we'll explore how to create a healthy tech-life balance that works for you.

## How to Create a Healthy Tech-Life Balance

Finding a balance between screen time and real-life activities is key to managing both your mental health and your PDA tendencies. Technology can be a great tool, but it's important to make sure it doesn't take over your life. Creating a healthy tech-life balance is about setting boundaries, being intentional with your screen time, and making sure you have time for offline activities that support your well-being.

One of the first steps in creating a healthy tech-life balance is **setting clear boundaries** around your screen time. This might involve limiting the amount of time you spend on certain apps or devices, or setting specific times of day when you allow yourself to use technology. For example, you might decide to only check social media after you've finished your homework or turn off your phone an hour before bed to help you wind down. By setting these boundaries, you can prevent screen time from becoming an all-consuming part of your day.

Another important aspect of balancing tech and life is **being intentional with your screen time**. Instead of mindlessly scrolling through social media or binge-watching shows for hours on end, try to be more mindful about how you use technology. Ask yourself, "Why am I using this right now? Is it helping me relax, connect with friends, or learn something new? Or am I using it to avoid something else?" Being more intentional with your screen time can help you make choices that support your mental health, rather than allowing technology to become a distraction from the things you need to address.

It's also helpful to **prioritize offline activities** that bring you joy and help you recharge. Whether it's going for a walk, reading a book, spending time with friends, or practicing a hobby, make sure you have time in your day for activities that don't involve screens. These offline activities are essential for maintaining a sense of balance and preventing burnout from too much digital stimulation. By creating a routine that includes time for both technology and offline activities, you'll feel more grounded and less overwhelmed by the demands of the digital world.

**Taking regular breaks** from technology is another important strategy for maintaining a healthy balance. Even short breaks can help reduce the mental fatigue that comes from staring at a screen for too long. Try the 20-20-20 rule: every 20 minutes, take a 20-second break to look at something 20 feet away. This simple practice can help reduce eye strain and give your brain a moment to reset, making it easier to stay focused and avoid getting lost in endless screen time.

Finally, consider creating **tech-free zones or times** in your day. This might mean designating certain areas of your home, like the dinner table or your bedroom, as screen-free spaces. It could also mean setting aside specific times of day when you completely disconnect from technology, such as during meals, before bed, or while spending time with family. These tech-free moments can help you reconnect with the real world and prevent technology from dominating your life.

By creating a healthy tech-life balance, you'll be able to enjoy the benefits of technology without letting it take over. In the next section, we'll explore how to navigate social media, which can be one of the most challenging aspects of the digital world for teens with PDA.

## Navigating Social Media Without Feeling Overloaded

Social media is a major part of life for many teens. It's a way to stay connected with friends, share experiences, and discover new things. But for teens with PDA, social media can also be a source of overwhelm. The constant notifications, the pressure to respond to messages, and the fear of missing out (FOMO) can create anxiety, making it difficult to enjoy the positive aspects of social media without feeling overloaded.

One of the biggest challenges of social media is the **pressure to always be connected**. Whether it's responding to messages, keeping up with your feed, or maintaining streaks on apps like Snapchat, the constant need to engage can make social media feel like a never-ending task. This pressure can lead to feelings of anxiety, especially when you feel like you're falling behind or missing out on important moments.

To navigate social media without feeling overloaded, it's important to **set boundaries** around your use of these platforms. Just like with screen time in general, setting limits on how often you check social media or how long you spend scrolling through your feed can help reduce the pressure to constantly be online. Consider turning off notifications for non-essential apps or setting specific times of day when you check social media, so it doesn't take over your entire day.

Another helpful strategy is to **curate your feed** to reduce overwhelm. Follow accounts that inspire you, make you feel good, or teach you something new, and unfollow or mute accounts that contribute to stress or negative feelings. Social media should be a space that uplifts and supports you, not one that adds to your anxiety. By curating your feed, you can create a digital environment that feels more positive and manageable.

It's also important to remember that **social media isn't real life**. It's easy to compare yourself to the perfect images and curated posts you see online, but remember that people only share the highlights of their lives on social media. Everyone has struggles and challenges that they don't post about, and comparing your real life to someone else's online persona is unrealistic. Focus on your own journey and remind yourself that social media is just a snapshot, not the whole picture.

When using social media, try to **engage mindfully**. Instead of mindlessly scrolling through posts, take the time to really connect with the content you're consuming. Ask yourself, "Is this adding value to my day? How is this making me feel?" If you notice that certain posts or platforms are making you feel anxious or overwhelmed, it might be time to take a break or adjust how you're engaging with them. Mindful engagement helps you stay in control of your social media use, rather than letting it control you.

Finally, don't be afraid to **take breaks from social media** when needed. It's okay to step away from your accounts for a while if you're feeling overwhelmed or anxious. Taking a break can give you the space to recharge and reset, so you can come back to social media with a clearer mind. Whether it's for a few hours, a day, or even longer, taking breaks can help you maintain a healthy relationship with social media.

By setting boundaries, curating your feed, and engaging mindfully, you can navigate social media in a way that feels positive and empowering, rather than overwhelming. In the next chapter, we'll dive into self-care strategies that actually work for teens with PDA, helping you recharge and find peace in a world full of demands.

# Chapter 13

# Self-Care Strategies that Actually Work

As a teen with Pathological Demand Avoidance (PDA), life can often feel like a constant balancing act of managing demands, anxiety, and overwhelming emotions. In the midst of trying to keep up with school, friendships, and family responsibilities, it's easy to forget about taking care of yourself. But self-care is not just about treating yourself to a break or indulging in things that make you happy—it's about intentionally making space to recharge, reset, and prioritize your mental and emotional well-being.

This chapter is all about self-care strategies that actually work for teens with PDA. We'll dive into what self-care really means for someone navigating PDA, provide practical tips you can incorporate into your daily life, and explore how you can find peace in a world full of demands. Self-care isn't just about bubble baths and face masks—it's about finding strategies that genuinely help you cope with stress, recharge your energy, and feel more grounded in your day-to-day life.

Let's start by understanding what self-care looks like specifically for teens with PDA and why it's such an essential part of managing your well-being.

## What Self-Care Really Means for PDA Teens

When you hear the term "self-care," you might think of activities like relaxation, pampering, or indulging in your favorite treats. While these can all be part of a self-care routine, true self-care goes much deeper. For teens with PDA, self-care is about creating a safe and supportive environment where you can manage the pressures and demands of life without feeling constantly overwhelmed. It's about actively taking steps to reduce stress, prioritize your mental health, and take control of how you respond to the demands you face.

Self-care for PDA teens often looks different from the typical "self-care" activities that are commonly talked about. Because demands can trigger anxiety, self-care might involve setting boundaries around how much you take on in a day or giving yourself permission to say no to things that feel overwhelming. It might mean structuring your day in a way that gives you plenty of downtime, without feeling guilty for not being "productive" all the time.

One of the biggest aspects of self-care for PDA teens is recognizing when you need to **step back** and recharge. Living with PDA often means that demands and social interactions can drain your energy faster than they do for others. It's important to listen to your body and mind and recognize when you're starting to feel overwhelmed. Taking regular breaks to recharge, whether that's through alone time, quiet activities, or engaging in something that soothes you, is an essential part of self-care.

Another important aspect of self-care for PDA teens is **creating routines** that work for you. Predictability and routine can help reduce the anxiety that comes with unexpected demands or changes in your environment. While it's not always possible to control every aspect of your day, having a general structure that you can rely on can help you feel more grounded. This might include setting aside time for relaxing activities, organizing your daily tasks, or creating rituals that help you transition from one part of your day to another.

Self-care also involves **self-compassion**—being kind to yourself when things don't go as planned. It's easy to get frustrated or feel guilty when you avoid tasks or struggle with demands, but self-care means recognizing that it's okay to take things at your own pace. You're doing the best you can, and it's important to be gentle with yourself, especially when things feel hard.

Finally, self-care for PDA teens means **building a support system**. Self-care doesn't mean you have to handle everything on your own. Having friends, family, or even a counselor who understands what you're going through can provide emotional support when you need it most. These relationships are part of your self-care routine, as they provide a space where you can share your struggles and feel understood without judgment.

Now that we understand what self-care really means for teens with PDA, let's explore some practical tips you can use to recharge and reset in your everyday life.

## Recharging and Resetting: Practical Tips for Every Day

Taking care of yourself on a daily basis is essential for managing the stress and demands that come with PDA. The following practical tips are designed to help you recharge and reset, so you can approach each day with a sense of calm and control.

1. **Create a Morning Routine that Grounds You**: Starting your day with a routine can help set the tone for the rest of the day. Try to create a morning routine that helps you feel grounded and centered before the demands of the day begin. This might involve something as simple as taking

a few minutes to breathe deeply, practicing mindfulness, or enjoying a quiet activity like reading or journaling. By starting your day with intention, you'll be better prepared to handle whatever comes your way.

2. **Use Timers to Break Tasks into Manageable Chunks**: When you're feeling overwhelmed by tasks or responsibilities, it can be helpful to use a timer to break the task down into smaller chunks. Set a timer for 10 or 15 minutes and focus on just one task during that time. When the timer goes off, take a short break and then reset the timer for another round. This technique helps prevent tasks from feeling too overwhelming and allows you to make steady progress without getting stuck in avoidance.

3. **Schedule Downtime**: Downtime is not a luxury—it's a necessity. Make sure you schedule regular breaks throughout your day to recharge. Whether it's a few minutes of quiet time between classes, a longer break after school, or time spent doing something you enjoy, scheduling downtime

ensures that you have the space to recharge without feeling guilty for stepping away from demands.

4. **Create a Calming Space**: Having a designated space where you can go to relax and unwind can make a big difference in your self-care routine. Whether it's your bedroom, a cozy corner in your house, or even a spot outside where you feel at peace, having a space that's just for you can help you recharge when you're feeling overwhelmed. Fill this space with things that soothe you, whether it's soft lighting, calming scents, or comforting objects.

5. **Practice Mindful Breathing**: When anxiety starts to build, taking a few moments to focus on your breathing can help calm your mind and body. Try the 4-7-8 breathing technique: breathe in for 4 seconds, hold the breath for 7 seconds, and exhale slowly for 8 seconds. Repeat this a few times to help reduce anxiety and bring yourself back to the present moment.

6. **Limit Overstimulation**: PDA teens are often sensitive to sensory input, so limiting overstimulation is an important part of self-care. If bright lights, loud noises, or too much social interaction are starting to feel overwhelming, take a step back and remove yourself from the environment if possible. Create moments of quiet and calm where you can reset without the constant sensory input that can drain your energy.

These tips are just a few ways you can incorporate self-care into your everyday routine. The key is to find what works for you and make self-care a priority, even on the busiest days. In the next section, we'll explore how to find peace in a world full of demands, so you can maintain a sense of calm and control no matter what life throws your way.

## Finding Peace in a World Full of Demands

Living with PDA often means feeling like the world is constantly demanding something from you. Whether it's schoolwork, chores, social commitments, or family expectations, it can feel like you're always under pressure to meet someone else's demands. But finding peace doesn't mean eliminating all demands—it's about learning how to navigate them in a way that allows you to stay calm and grounded.

One of the first steps to finding peace in a world full of demands is learning to **manage your expectations**—both your own and those of others. It's easy to feel overwhelmed when you set high expectations for yourself or when others place unrealistic demands on you. By managing your expectations, you can create a sense of balance. Ask yourself, "What can I realistically handle today?" and adjust your to-do list accordingly. It's okay to take things one step at a time and prioritize tasks that feel manageable.

Another important strategy is to **focus on what you can control**. In a world full of demands, it's easy to feel like everything is outside of your control, but there are always things you can manage. You might not be able to control the demands others place on you, but you can control how you respond to them. Whether it's setting boundaries, asking for more time, or breaking tasks into smaller pieces, focusing on what you can control helps reduce the feeling of being overwhelmed.

**Mindfulness** is another powerful tool for finding peace. When you're feeling stressed or anxious about demands, practicing mindfulness can help bring you back to the present moment. Mindfulness is about focusing on what's happening right now, without worrying about the past or the future. Whether it's through deep breathing, meditation, or simply paying attention to your senses, mindfulness helps quiet the mental noise and bring a sense of calm to your day.

**Letting go of perfectionism** is also key to finding peace. When you're constantly striving for perfection, every task feels like a mountain to climb. But perfectionism only adds to the pressure, making it harder to get started or finish tasks. Instead of aiming for perfection, focus on progress. Celebrate the small steps you take each day, and remember that it's okay to make mistakes. You're doing the best you can, and that's enough.

Finally, finding peace means **giving yourself permission to say no**. It's okay to turn down invitations, decline additional tasks, or step away from activities that feel too overwhelming. Saying no is not a failure—it's a form of self-care that allows you to protect your energy and focus on what truly matters. By setting boundaries and giving yourself permission to say no, you create space for peace and calm in your life.

# Chapter 14

# Growing Pains – Coping with Transitions and Uncertainty

Life is full of changes, big and small, and as a teen with Pathological Demand Avoidance (PDA), these transitions can feel particularly overwhelming. Whether it's moving to a new school, transitioning from middle school to high school, or even navigating daily changes in your routine, coping with transitions can stir up a mix of emotions—anxiety, fear, frustration, and sometimes even excitement. While uncertainty and change are natural parts of life, they often feel like looming challenges for someone with PDA, as the unpredictability of change can trigger stress and avoidance behaviors.

This chapter will help you face transitions head-on, without letting fear or anxiety take control. We'll explore why changes, both big and small, feel so overwhelming, and how you can develop the flexibility and resilience needed to cope with life's constant shifts. By learning to handle transitions with confidence, you can move through the growing pains of life without feeling like you're being knocked off balance every time something new comes your way.

Let's start by looking at how you can face life's changes without fear, so that transitions become something you can manage rather than something to dread.

## Facing Changes Head-On Without Fear

Change is inevitable, but for teens with PDA, it can often feel like a looming threat. The unpredictability of transitions, whether it's a shift in your daily routine or a big life change like moving or graduating, can trigger intense feelings of anxiety and avoidance. But facing changes head-on doesn't have to be terrifying—it's about learning how to approach transitions with curiosity, flexibility, and a sense of control.

The first step in facing changes without fear is recognizing that **fear of the unknown is natural**.

Everyone, not just people with PDA, feels a sense of discomfort when faced with uncertainty. It's okay to feel anxious or worried about transitions, but it's important not to let that fear take control. Acknowledge your feelings and remind yourself that it's normal to be uncertain, but that uncertainty doesn't have to stop you from moving forward.

One of the biggest reasons transitions feel so overwhelming is because they often represent a loss of control. For someone with PDA, who thrives on predictability and routine, change can feel like a threat to your sense of stability. To face transitions without fear, it's important to **find ways to regain control** in the midst of change. This might involve breaking down the transition into smaller, more manageable steps. For example, if you're starting at a new school, focus on one aspect of the change at a time—getting familiar with your new schedule, meeting your teachers, or learning the layout of the building. By breaking the transition down into smaller pieces, you can approach each step with more confidence.

Another key to facing change head-on is **reframing how you think about transitions**. Instead of viewing change as something negative or frightening, try to see it as an opportunity for growth and new experiences. While it's natural to feel anxious about the unknown, transitions can also open up new possibilities and help you develop new skills. When you shift your mindset from fear to curiosity, you give yourself permission to explore the opportunities that come with change.

It's also helpful to **prepare for transitions in advance**. When you know a change is coming, take time to mentally and emotionally prepare for it. This might involve creating a plan for how you'll handle the transition or talking to someone you trust about your feelings. The more prepared you feel, the less overwhelming the change will seem. If the transition is unexpected, give yourself permission to take things one step at a time and ask for support when you need it.

Finally, facing change without fear means **being kind to yourself during the process**. Transitions are hard, and it's okay if you don't handle them perfectly. Allow yourself to feel the emotions that come with change—whether it's anxiety, frustration, or even excitement—and remind yourself that it's okay to take things at your own pace. By approaching transitions with self-compassion, you'll be better equipped to navigate the challenges that come your way.

## How to Handle Life's Big (and Small) Transitions

Life is full of transitions, from the big changes like moving to a new city or starting high school, to the smaller daily transitions like adjusting to a new class schedule or a change in plans. For teens with PDA, both big and small transitions can feel equally overwhelming. However, by developing strategies to handle these changes, you can move through them with more ease and less stress.

One of the most important strategies for handling transitions is to **embrace flexibility**. Life is unpredictable, and trying to control every aspect of a transition is often impossible. Instead of resisting change, practice going with the flow and adapting to new circumstances as they arise. This doesn't mean you have to love every change that comes your way, but it does mean finding ways to adjust and make the best of the situation. For example, if your plans change unexpectedly, focus on what you can do in the moment rather than fixating on what didn't go according to plan.

Another helpful strategy is to **create a sense of continuity** during transitions. For teens with PDA, routine and predictability are essential for managing anxiety, so when a big change disrupts your usual routine, it can feel destabilizing. To cope with this, try to maintain some elements of your routine even during transitions. This might involve sticking to a morning or evening routine that grounds you, or finding small rituals that provide a sense of familiarity in the midst of change. Having these anchors in your day can help you feel more stable, even when everything else feels uncertain.

**Breaking down transitions into smaller steps** is another effective way to manage both big and small changes. When you're faced with a major life transition, like moving to a new home or starting a new school, it can feel overwhelming to tackle everything at once. Instead, break the transition down into manageable steps and focus on one thing at a time. For example, if you're moving, start by packing one room or focusing on one task each day. By breaking the transition into smaller pieces, you make it more manageable and less intimidating.

When it comes to smaller transitions, like changes in your daily routine, **preparing yourself mentally and emotionally** can make a big difference. For example, if you know your class schedule is going to change or if you have a busy day ahead, take a few moments to plan how you'll navigate the day. Consider what strategies you can use to stay calm and focused, and give yourself permission to take breaks when needed. By preparing for these smaller transitions, you reduce the likelihood of feeling overwhelmed by the unexpected.

**Seeking support from others** is another important strategy for handling transitions. You don't have to navigate change on your own—friends, family members, and counselors can provide valuable support during times of transition. Whether it's talking through your feelings, getting advice, or simply having someone to listen, reaching out for support can make the process of transition feel less isolating and more manageable.

Finally, remember that **transitions are opportunities for growth**. While change can be uncomfortable, it's also a chance to learn more about yourself and develop new skills. Each transition you navigate successfully builds your resilience and confidence, helping you handle future changes with greater ease. By approaching transitions with an open mind and a willingness to grow, you can turn even the most challenging changes into opportunities for personal development.

## Developing Flexibility in a World That's Always Changing

Flexibility is one of the most valuable skills you can develop, especially in a world that's constantly changing. For teens with PDA, the idea of being flexible might feel uncomfortable, as predictability and control are often key to managing anxiety. However, developing flexibility doesn't mean giving up control entirely—it means learning how to adapt to changes in a way that feels manageable and empowering.

The first step in developing flexibility is to **practice letting go of perfectionism**. One of the reasons change feels so overwhelming for teens with PDA is because it disrupts the sense of control you have over your environment. Perfectionism—the need to have everything go exactly as planned—can make transitions feel even more stressful. By letting go of the need for everything to be perfect, you open yourself up to the possibility that things might not go as expected, and that's okay. Embrace the idea that things can still turn out well, even if they don't go exactly according to plan.

Another important aspect of flexibility is **developing a mindset of curiosity**. Instead of approaching changes with fear or resistance, try to approach them with a sense of curiosity. Ask yourself, "What can I learn from this situation?" or "How can I make the most of this change?" By shifting your mindset from one of anxiety to one of curiosity, you'll find it easier to adapt to new circumstances and explore the opportunities that come with change.

**Building resilience through small changes** is another way to develop flexibility. You don't have to wait for a major life transition to practice being flexible—start with smaller changes in your daily routine. For example, if your usual plans change or something unexpected comes up, practice going with the flow and adapting to the new situation. The more you practice flexibility in small ways, the more confident you'll become in your ability to handle bigger transitions.

It's also helpful to **develop coping strategies** for when things don't go as planned. Flexibility doesn't mean that change will always feel easy—it's natural to feel anxious or frustrated when things don't go the way you expected. Having a set of coping strategies, such as mindfulness exercises, breathing techniques, or talking to someone you trust, can help you manage your emotions and stay calm when things feel uncertain.

Another key to developing flexibility is **focusing on the things you can control**. While change often involves elements that are outside of your control, there are always aspects of a situation that you can manage. Whether it's how you respond to the change, how you organize your time, or how you take care of yourself during the transition, focusing on what you can control helps you feel more grounded and less overwhelmed by the uncertainty.

Finally, remember that **flexibility is a skill that takes time to develop**. You don't have to become perfectly flexible overnight—it's a process that requires practice and patience. Each time you face a change, whether it's big or small, remind yourself that you're building your flexibility muscle. With time, you'll become more confident in your ability to handle life's transitions and adapt to the unexpected with grace and resilience.

# Conclusion

As you reach the end of this book, you've likely learned a lot about yourself, about PDA, and about how to navigate the world around you with confidence. It hasn't been easy—understanding Pathological Demand Avoidance and managing its challenges during your teenage years takes real strength. But if there's one thing that's become clear, it's this: **you've got this**. You have the power, the resilience, and the unique perspective to build a future that works for you. This chapter is all about embracing that path forward, feeling empowered by what you've learned, and knowing that you are capable of overcoming whatever challenges life throws your way.

Your journey doesn't stop here—this is just the beginning. Whether you're feeling ready to take on the world or still uncertain about the road ahead, this chapter will give you the encouragement and reassurance you need to trust in yourself and your abilities. You don't need to have everything figured out, and it's okay if there are still things that feel hard or confusing. What's important is that you've taken the time to understand yourself better, and that understanding will serve as a foundation for everything that comes next.

Let's start by talking about how you can build a future that works for you—one that's filled with opportunities, joy, and success on your own terms.

## You've Got This! Building a Future That Works for You

Building a future that works for you doesn't mean following someone else's roadmap. It doesn't mean meeting all the expectations that society or others may place on you. Instead, it's about carving out a path that fits your needs, your strengths, and your dreams. As a teen with PDA, you may feel like you have to navigate life differently from others—and that's completely okay. In fact, the way you approach life can be one of your greatest strengths.

The first step to building a future that works for you is to **embrace your individuality**. You are unique, and so is your journey. The challenges you face because of PDA may make certain aspects of life more difficult, but they also provide you with a deep understanding of yourself and your limits. Instead of viewing these challenges as obstacles, try to see them as opportunities to learn more about what works for you. When you embrace who you are, including your sensitivities and needs, you give yourself the freedom to design a future that aligns with your values and aspirations.

It's also important to **define success on your own terms**. Success doesn't have to look the same for everyone. For some, it might mean pursuing a specific career path, while for others, it might mean building meaningful relationships or maintaining a healthy balance between work and personal life. What does success mean to you? Take some time to reflect on what truly matters to you—what makes you feel fulfilled and happy? By defining success for yourself, you can set goals that feel achievable and aligned with your own desires, rather than trying to live up to someone else's expectations.

Another key aspect of building a future that works for you is learning how to **balance ambition with self-care**. It's natural to want to achieve great things, but it's important to remember that your mental health and well-being come first. Living with PDA means that certain demands can trigger anxiety, so it's crucial to build a life where you can pursue your goals without feeling constantly overwhelmed. This might mean creating routines that allow for plenty of downtime, setting boundaries around work or social commitments, or learning to say no when a situation feels too stressful. You don't have to push yourself to the brink to be successful—true success comes from finding balance.

In addition to balancing ambition with self-care, you'll also need to develop **flexibility and adaptability**. Life is unpredictable, and things won't always go according to plan. But that's okay. Being flexible means being able to adjust when things change, to go with the flow when necessary, and to not be too hard on yourself when setbacks occur. Flexibility doesn't mean giving up on your goals—it means being open to new possibilities and trusting that you have the strength to handle whatever comes your way.

Finally, building a future that works for you means **surrounding yourself with the right support system**. You don't have to do this alone. Whether it's friends, family, teachers, or mentors, having people in your corner who understand your needs and believe in you can make all the difference. These are the people who will lift you up when you're feeling down, celebrate your victories, and remind you that you are capable of achieving great things. By building a strong support system, you'll have the encouragement and guidance you need to move forward with confidence.

As you come to the end of this book, it's important to take a moment to acknowledge just how far you've come. Whether you've been living with PDA for a while or are still coming to terms with what it means for you, navigating this journey takes incredible strength. The fact that you've taken the time to learn more about yourself, to understand how PDA impacts your life, and to develop strategies for managing it is something to be proud of. This isn't an easy journey, but you've shown that you are capable of facing it head-on.

One of the most important things to remember as you continue your PDA journey is that **there's no "right" way to live with PDA.** Everyone's experience is different, and what works for one person might not work for another. The key is to find what works for you, to honor your needs, and to be kind to yourself along the way. You don't have to meet every demand perfectly, and you don't have to have everything figured out. It's okay to make mistakes, to take things slow, and to ask for help when you need it. You are doing your best, and that is more than enough.

Another piece of encouragement is to **trust in your ability to grow and adapt**. PDA might feel overwhelming at times, and there may be moments when it seems like everything is too much. But you've already proven that you can handle tough situations, even when they feel impossible. Every time you face a challenge, you're building resilience, and that resilience will serve you well as you move forward. You don't have to be fearless to be brave—just showing up and doing the best you can is an act of courage.

As you continue to navigate your teenage years and beyond, it's also important to remember that **it's okay to ask for help**. You don't have to do everything on your own, and reaching out for support is a sign of strength, not weakness. Whether it's talking to a trusted friend, seeking guidance from a therapist, or leaning on your family for support, asking for help when you need it will make your journey easier. You are not alone in this—there are people who care about you and want to see you succeed.

Finally, remember to **celebrate your victories**, no matter how small they may seem. Living with PDA means that some days will be harder than others, and sometimes even getting through the day is an accomplishment in itself. Take the time to acknowledge the progress you've made, whether it's completing a task that once felt impossible, standing up for yourself in a difficult situation, or simply taking care of your mental health. Every step forward is worth celebrating, and those small victories will add up over time.

As you move forward on your journey, know that you have the strength, the courage, and the tools to build a life that feels right for you. There will be ups and downs, but with each challenge you face, you'll grow stronger and more confident in your ability to handle whatever comes your way. Trust in yourself, be patient with your progress, and remember that you've got this.